DEMOCRATS 101

Democrats

★ 101 ★

A PRIMER FOR US

J.M. PURVIS

PLAINWORDS PRESS

Library of Congress Control Number: 2021918265

ISBN: 978-1-7372513-0-9
eBook ISBN: 978-1-7372513-1-6

First Edition 2021

Printed in the United States of America

Design by Mark Melnick

PLAINWORDS PRESS
85 Eastern Parkway, Suite 1A, Brooklyn, NY 11238
www.plainwordspress.com

This is not a traditional book.

It's not about election campaigns or political positions, and it's not about policies or grand theories. It's about us. It's about you and me, the real Democratic Party. It's about our basic values and our long search for identity, and why that is now the most important issue we face.

★

One person wrote the book you're about to read, but fellow Democrats from every corner of our tent helped shape its ideas. Each and every one of those people is united by their frustration with our current state of affairs, and their deep conviction that what we do in the coming years matters enormously.

Contents

★

The Question   11

How We Got Here
  The Prime Directive   19
  The Endless Curse   27
  Unraveling   30
  Birth of the Death Star   39
  Over the Cliff   50
  Blood in the Water   54

Us
  The Common Thread   57
  Emotion versus Reason   63
  The End of Norman Rockwell   66
  Back to the Beginning   74
  Race   80

Them
  Who Are These People Anyway?   89
  The Dark Empire   104

Myths and Fables   114

The Democratic Creed   127

Tomorrow . . .   131

Ten Questions We Need to Ask Ourselves   137

•

Notes & Image Credits   139

Acknowledgments   140

Resources   142

About the Author   143

DEMOCRATS 101

The Question

★

What, exactly, is a Democrat?

You, me, all of us . . . why do we belong to the same party? What ties us all together . . . ranchers in Montana and laborers in Miami and single moms in Los Angeles? Who, in fact, are we?

Here's a better question: Why do we think we know? Why are we all so damn sure we know who we are when we can't spell it out? You think you can? Try it. Take out a pen and make an actual list: What beliefs define every Democrat in this country? What do we all hold dear, every single one of us, from rural Joe Manchin supporters in West Virginia to fierce Alexandria Ocasio-Cortez backers in the Bronx, and everyone in between? If we're all in the same party, then we must all share some kind of core belief system, and we ought to know what it is. If we don't, if our plan is to keep on arguing about it endlessly and leave the Republicans to apply the labels, that should scare the hell out of us. Especially now.

Of course, some people would say we're Democrats because we're not Republicans. We live in a two-party system in this country, and you do really have to choose one or the other. Even independents and Libertarians have to make that choice in the end. It's a valid reason to vote Democrat . . . especially these days . . . but it isn't a very good reason to *be* a Democrat.

Policy damned sure isn't the reason. If policy was what defined us, the Democratic Party would have disintegrated a long time ago. We have never agreed on policy, and we never will. Ever. Yet, we seem obsessed with policy as if it were the end-all, the one battle worth having, the very essence of who we are. Health care is a great example. How much time and emotion have we wasted on that issue? How many litmus tests have we created?[1] Medicare for all versus a better Obamacare isn't about who we are. The idea of health care for everyone? Even that doesn't define who we are. We support health care for everyone *because* of who we are. That's what's important. It's what separates us from the Republican Party, and it's at the heart of what's been missing in the way we approach things.

Policy is about how to fix things. Issues are about what needs fixing. Our core beliefs are something else entirely. Our core values are not "left" or "right." They can't be, not if they're central to all of us. And they're not about

---

[1] And how many attack ads have we helped the Republicans create?

the issues or events of the moment. As emotional as we may get over these things, words like "moderate" and "progressive" don't define who we are. They define how we approach policy. They define how we want to get things done. Core beliefs, on the other hand, define us as Democrats, and we need . . . desperately . . . to recognize that. If 2016 wasn't a wake-up call, then the blue wave that didn't come in 2020 sure ought to be, to say nothing of the right-wing mob that stormed the Capitol.

The Republican Party understands core identity perfectly. Nowadays, being a Republican is a brand. What they're selling is power and how to hold on to it—control. Their messaging . . . and their values . . . is whatever works.

We can't do that. Our "product" is our beliefs, what we stand for, our basic identity. Failing to understand that . . . failing to define it . . . is why so much of our messaging doesn't work.

We talk endlessly about how diverse we are—the big tent. And it's true. We can be found in almost every imaginable part of the country. We represent just about every demographic that exists—every age group, every race, you name it. We *are* everybody, so why the hell does the Republican Party . . . the bad guys . . . get away with so much? Why do they get away with selling fake populism when we're the ones supporting what people actually need? Why do they get away with smearing us and our initiatives . . . and all we seem to do is go on squabbling? Aren't you tired of it? Aren't you frustrated? We all sense that bigger things are at stake, especially now, so why can't we ever seem to communicate that? Why are we always playing catch-up?

This country was founded on certain ideals, basic principles that were revolutionary at the time. These ideals were implied promises. Those promises were imperfect, to be sure, and they faced huge opposition. And they certainly did *not* apply to everyone. But they made their mark. Over time, they took hold and evolved, just as surely as the country evolved. Social change is traditionally slow. So is social progress. A good ninety years went by before America managed to abolish slavery.[2] It was another five decades before women gained the right to vote. But the direction of that progress has been inexorable, and with technology on the scene, that progress has begun moving at an ever-increasing rate.

The modern Democratic Party, the one we know as ours, has been an integral part of that basic struggle for social progress. Not always, and often not by so many of us, but at the moments of real progress in this country, it's always been Democrats who were there. It's been Democrats who spoke out, and it's been because of our

---

2 The Thirteenth Amendment, January 31,
1865. See the movie *Lincoln* for more.

steadily evolving core values. The basic thread has always been there. It's been buried in our moral fabric since the very beginning, but for a long time the social norms of this country wouldn't allow us to recognize those values as a party. Too many people . . . too many of us . . . were still in thrall to the traditions and prejudices of the past.

And that's exactly why right now . . . these next few years . . . is a unique moment in history. Social norms are beginning to catch up to our inherent values. Not everywhere, of course, or Donald Trump wouldn't have been elected president. But enough, enough to launch huge Black Lives Matter protests across the nation, enough to do a lot of things.

And it's recent. It's easy to forget just how new so many of these attitudes are—their extent, their acceptance—and it isn't just about race. The majority of Americans no longer view gay marriage as an issue, and that's a historic first. Harvey Weinstein fell, and #MeToo is real. More than 60 percent of Americans think the federal government should ensure universal health care.

This is a seismic shift in the norms of this country.[3] It's a move toward a deeper realization of those revolutionary ideals America was founded on, and it's going on everywhere—in the media, in education, and in day-to-day life itself.

---

3 The Trump-inspired backlash notwithstanding.

But it's confusing. Age-old truths and traditions are crashing for an awful lot of people. Unsettling issues are springing up in their place, issues . . . injustices . . . that so many Americans never had to think about before, things like transgender bathrooms and renaming famous military bases and the idea that racism really is everywhere. It may be crystal clear for some of us, but for an enormous chunk of America, it's unsettling. And that has spawned wild conspiracy theories, "alternative facts," and a deluge of more information than anybody can digest. Huge numbers of people don't quite know what to believe, and it's not just Republican voters. There's a growing hunger among an enormous number of people for values and direction, for someone to make sense of the very new world we seem to be headed into at light speed.

Manipulating that hunger is how Donald Trump became president. Not understanding it is a big chunk of why Hillary lost, why the 2020 blue wave never came, and if we're not careful, it'll be why we lose again. America is in the early stages of a vast political upheaval, one that's going to last decades. Trump is just the tip of the iceberg, a passing facet of what's playing out. What's coming in the next twenty years is nothing short of a colossal shift in the way we live and think and vote.

And that's why we need to do more than just win elections. Our goal is a just society for every American, and to do that, we need our values to prevail. If we want to make sure we never ever have to fight over the concept of basic human rights again, then we have to make sure people understand just what those rights are. They need to understand, and they need to believe.

We don't accomplish that by toppling our opponents. We accomplish that by including our opponents. Not the haters, not the conspiracy-ranters, but the others . . . the millions and millions of Americans who aren't really sure what's going on. These are the people we need to win over, and we need to do it bit by bit, year by year. And that's why we need to become the standard-bearers for the kinds of basic values that just ring true.

What we need now is a clear statement of our beliefs, something in simple, direct English that rings true to everyone in this country . . . Black, White, Hispanic, techies and coal miners, everyone . . . basic values that are truly universal, that can serve as a moral compass as we struggle through all the very complex problems headed our way.

The first step in writing out those beliefs is to take a long, hard look at ourselves. We Democrats carry blame, because the mess we're in is not an accident. The Tea Party wasn't an accident. Trump wasn't an accident. None of it was . . . none of it is . . . and we've played a part, all of us, from establishment bigwigs down to the most humble voter. The Republican Party may be the villain, but we've helped dig the hole we're in, and we're not going to get out of it until we face up to exactly what has happened.

As Americans, we have a very short historical memory. If it didn't happen recently, it can't be important. Well, in this case, it is. Every bit of what we face today as Democrats is tied directly to our history as a party . . . every problem, every passion, every possible solution. If we want to fix things, if we truly want to succeed, then we need to understand exactly how we got here.

How We Got Here

★

THE PRIME DIRECTIVE

We began life the day Franklin Roosevelt was inaugurated in 1933. There was nothing before, everything after, a truly remarkable turning point in American politics that still touches us today . . . though most of us are only dimly aware.

America was different in 1933. For one thing, the country was White. Physically. Most states outside the South were at least 95 percent White.[4] Union workers in factories were overwhelmingly White. Most farmers were White. Soldiers in the army were White.[5] And they were men. White men ruled everything . . . business, religion, politics, all of it. Women had only had the vote for twelve years, and people were still getting used to it. There were exactly eight women in Congress. Professional work for educated women was virtually unavail-

---

4 The 1930 US Census.

5 The Buffalo Soldiers were among several notable
. . . and little-known . . . exceptions.

able. Education itself was difficult (Harvard wouldn't admit its first female medical student until 1945).

Jews were all but outcasts to most Americans back then . . . or worse (in 1939, a Roper poll found that only 39 percent of Americans thought Jews should be treated like other people). Hispanics virtually didn't exist. The 1930 US Census lists the "Mexican" population at 1.2 percent. Native Americans made up 0.3 percent, and Asian Americans even less.

Of course there were Black Americans in those days, nearly twelve million, but in many ways, they were invisible as well. The majority lived under Jim Crow in the South,[6] which meant they couldn't vote or get a proper education, let alone a decent job. Up North, everything was segregated de facto, and police violence was widespread. In the Midwest and elsewhere, sunset towns[7]—a quaint term that isn't so quaint at all—were common. Racism wasn't a "problem" in 1933; it was the social norm for most White Americans, Southern or Northern. This picture (right), taken in Marion, Indiana, in 1930, says it all:

---

6 Mississippi was almost half Black.

7 A "sunset town" or "sundown town" was a town or neighborhood that was purposely all White. The term came from prominent signs that said "colored people" (frequently the N-word was used) had to leave town by sundown. Yep, they really existed and not so long ago.

Lynching of Thomas Shipp and Abram Smith, August 7, 1930.

———

Life for White folks was different, too. There was no middle class as we know it today, no vast suburbs with neat green lawns and indoor garages. Forty percent of all Americans still lived a rural life on farms, or in very small towns.[8] That's nearly half the country. And 90 percent of those farms had no electricity. Out in the fields on those farms, horses were still pulling most of the plows, and the cows were milked by hand.

———

8 Statistics from the 1930 census.

In the cities, tenements were rampant, and hunger. Labor unions were violently suppressed and child labor was still around. Child labor. Less than ninety years ago. And the kids in those factories and mines weren't working forty-hour workweeks, either. Nobody was. The eight-hour day hadn't been invented. Neither had the five-day workweek. You worked as long as you had to and got paid whatever the employer decided. There was no workers' comp, no employer-sponsored health insurance. If something happened to you, that was your problem.

Franklin Roosevelt changed all that. He arrived like an earthquake, creating programs like Social Security and the National Labor Relations Board. He established a minimum wage and standard working hours and federally insured savings accounts, an incredible number of social programs that, one way or the other, touched almost everyone . . . programs that even Republican politicians now take for granted.

He also created a sense of national community among an enormous swath of working people, something no one had ever done before. He inspired, and he made them believe. He spoke to the country as a whole, regardless of their political party. He said things like, "We are going to make a country in which no one is left out," and, "Let us never forget that government is ourselves," and, "We all go up or else all go down as one people." He said these things often, everywhere, all across the country. He was tireless at delivering the message about common people and government . . . the new government, their government. He gave people a sense of their better selves, of being one. He gave people a sense of hope. And in so doing, he created us . . . the modern Democratic Party.

Over time, the New Deal became wildly popular. It transformed America,[9] and it was Roosevelt who made it happen. It was Roosevelt who altered our very sense of ourselves as a country, lifted us up. And when he died, people wept.

Of course, Republican politicians and the wealthy who supported them were appalled. They fought Roosevelt's activism tooth and nail . . . they still do . . . but Roosevelt's activist philosophy survived. It thrived, and it's the essence of our party today . . . whether you're moderate, progressive, or anything else. That activist philosophy is why we have Medicaid and Medicare and the Centers for Disease Control and Prevention.[10] It's why we have an interstate highway system, ingredients labeled on food, and clean drinking water. That activ-

---

9 There were other factors, big ones like the Great Depression and World War II, but the influence of Roosevelt is undeniable.

10 The Centers for Disease Control and Prevention . . . the CDC.

ism is the foundation for almost everything we take for granted about modern life.[11]

This is the single most radical concept of Roosevelt's entire Presidency, and the center of our struggle today: **the idea that the American government exists to help the people**. He taught that endlessly, everywhere, that the federal government's sole reason for being was to protect American citizens and actively promote their welfare.

That was a revolutionary idea in 1933. It's hard to imagine today, but back then, a lot of people considered it heresy. "The business of America is business" was an apt saying. Big business ran the country, and it ran politics as well. People like Rockefeller and Ford and J. P. Morgan not only lived lives of incredible luxury, they owned many of the politicians, and there was nothing subtle about it. Those business moguls set policies behind the scenes, and few dared oppose them. Unregulated capitalism was the order of the day . . . what was good for big business was good for the country (sound familiar?). Rugged individualism was the order of the day, too. If you weren't rich, it was your own fault.

The concept of rugged individualism was a philosophy built in colonial times, pioneer days when 95 per-

---

11 Teddy Roosevelt deserves a lot of credit for earlier changes as well, but that's a different story.

cent of us lived in rural areas, when many of us grew our own food, and help was self-help.[12] When the Founding Fathers got together, most people had to walk if they wanted to go anywhere (unless you had a horse),[13] and it was an era when people from another state were considered foreigners. Modern medicine and supermarkets didn't exist. The idea of a country as we know it didn't even exist, let alone the idea of a modern national government that stretched out from the Atlantic Seaboard into what was then the vast unknown. This, then, was the world the United States Constitution was written in.

By 1933, that pioneer world had mostly disappeared. The Industrial Revolution had engulfed America, along with giant corporations and assembly lines. World War I had happened and America had become a mighty power, but despite all that change, the original philosophy of limited government from the 1700s had never been challenged in a meaningful way.[14]

Roosevelt not only challenged it, he destroyed it forever, a fact that will not change in its essence no mat-

---

12 Unless, of course, you were a slave.

13 The time it took delegates to travel by horse back and forth from their state capitals . . . there were no telephones . . . was a big factor in how long it took to write the Constitution.

14 The Civil War and its aftermath and Teddy Roosevelt being major exceptions.

ter how hard the Republicans continue to fight it. That is the first legacy Roosevelt left us, and it has served as our Prime Directive to this very day: **the idea that the Democratic Party exists to better people's lives, that we are not just out to hold office but to make America a better country to live in**. That is no small thing.

And Roosevelt did this without ideology. He had no coherent political philosophy; both liberals and conservatives served in his first cabinet. But he did have a strong practical philosophy. His job . . . what he saw as his purpose . . . was to better the lives of ordinary Americans and save us all from the Great Depression, and to that end he would try anything, any program, as long as it worked. His only real criterion was that it helped the working class that was his coalition: the White factory workers and Black Americans and Catholics and immigrants who were the building blocks of his base. That working-class coalition and the programs to better their day-to-day lives became his end-all.

And this is Roosevelt's second legacy to us, an idea that has shaped our party for the past seven decades and still troubles us today: that our political future is tied to a specific, traditional coalition, with the predominately White working class and Black Americans at its core. This underlying assumption . . . and the endless policies we feed it . . . has never left our collective subconscious. Keeping this ghost alive . . . the unconscious image of

FDR's coalition and its electoral power[15] . . . has been our holy grail, an incessant quest that is the real origin of identity politics, which . . . whether we want to admit it or not . . . we still follow.

THE ENDLESS CURSE

Roosevelt's presidency had a dark side as well, a malignant undercurrent that has dogged our footsteps ever since.

That dark side was slavery, and its shadow still hung over the country in 1933, quite literally. Tens of thousands of Confederate soldiers were still alive at that point,[16] and their offspring were in office. White segregationists had not only taken over the South again, they had rewritten its history as well, rewritten reality. Slavery was no longer the cause of the Civil War in this new telling, states' rights were. The Confederacy was transformed into a noble struggle almost overnight. Up North, White children learned to sing "Dixie" in school, and the Confederate flag itself became a symbol of a heroic Lost Cause, a mythic place where some-

---

15 Power that gave us forty-eight years in the Senate and sixty-two years in the House, with the exception of short periods under Truman and Eisenhower.

16 And tens of thousands of former slaves.

how a lot of slaves had been happy and the Good Master protected them.[17]

As modern Democrats, it's easy for us to forget that there was once another Democratic Party, a strong national party, and that it supported slavery. From 1844 on, and from even before that, the hard core of that party whose name we still carry fought tooth and nail to maintain their slaves. In 1861, that same hard core of Democrats became the Confederacy. After the war, they became Democrats once again; Democrat slaveholders turning into Democrat segregationists. And once the segregationists took back control of the South, all the Southern members of Congress became Democrats overnight . . . White segregationist Democrats. And our curse began.

It was called "the Solid South" . . . "Dixiecrats" in polite society . . . officials who were reelected over and over again, often until death or senility overcame them.[18] And because Congress worked on a seniority system in those days, these same White segregationists came to control most of the powerful Senate and House commit-

---

17 If you're thinking all this is "old history," ponder just when we started debunking the Lost Cause myth. The Confederate flag on the South Carolina statehouse didn't come down until 2015. The idea that US Army bases shouldn't be named after Confederate generals is much more recent.

tees, which meant that for the entire New Deal and long beyond, they held a heavy hand over the flow of legislation. They had the power to veto just about anything, and that fact became FDR's personal marriage with the devil, and that made it ours as well.

No one will ever know what FDR's private feelings on race really were. He certainly took major steps toward bettering the condition of Black Americans. Though segregation was rampant, he included them in his back-to-work programs. Jobs were created. And he outlawed discrimination in the federal government, at least on paper. Most of all, at Eleanor's urging, he spoke to them. And that was enough to move the entire Black American vote from the party of Lincoln to the Democrats.

But in the end, FDR always caved to the political reality he faced. He spoke eloquently to the nation as a whole, and he spoke directly to the workingman, but he never took a meaningful public stand on things like racial equality or universal justice. Those were cans he kicked very far down the road, all the way to where they lie at our feet today.

---

18 Senator Strom Thurmond of South Carolina served until he was one hundred years old. His younger self was quoted as saying, "there's not enough troops in the army to force the Southern people to break down segregation and admit the Negro race into our theaters, into our swimming pools, into our homes, and into our churches."

UNRAVELING

A cultural shock wave hit this country in the 1950s and '60s. It literally tore open our party, wounded it so thoroughly that it stills plagues us today.

For a long time after World War II, most people thought America was sailing along. We were the new superpower. We were winners, and the country was full of good-paying jobs and unions and worker benefits no one had ever had before. There were supermarkets and two-car garages, and cute little kids riding their bicycles around endlessly expanding suburbs full of new schools and churches. It seemed idyllic, full of promise. Of course, that idyllic sense of promise only existed if you were White.

More than a million Black Americans served in uniform during the war, many of them overseas. They worked hard and sacrificed like all the other servicemen, but when they came back home, they didn't get a hero's welcome. They didn't get good jobs, either. They got Jim Crow . . . again . . . the same menial, dead-end jobs and daily humiliation, the same threats of beatings and lynchings they'd had before. It was as if nothing had happened, as if those Black soldiers had never gone off and served, and it didn't sit very well.

Sporadic protests broke out in the South. It was nothing White America noticed . . . nothing we Democrats noticed . . . but Black communities did. Things were simmering, and then there was a whiff of change in the air. In 1947, Jackie Robinson became the first Black American to play major league baseball, a star that everyone could read about in the papers, a hero to look up to. In 1948, Truman ordered the integration of the military, and even if the military didn't carry it out, Truman's act was noticed by every Black American in the country.

But the truly revolutionary events happened in the fifties and early sixties, and they were revolutionary because, for the first time, they didn't just happen to Black Americans. Television had appeared,[19] and suddenly Jim Crow and all its ugliness began to "happen" to all of us. Rosa Parks sat on a bus in Montgomery, Alabama, and the result was presented to us on national television over dinner.[20] So was the violence when Little Rock High School was integrated by the Eighty-Second Airborne, and the lunch counter sit-ins, and the armed conflict between White segregationists and US Marshals that broke out at the University of Mississippi. Two people died in that all-night shootout, more than

---

19 By 1955, more than half of households had one. Before 1950, most people didn't even know what it was.

20 Once upon a time, families all watched the nightly news on network television at 6:30 p.m.

three hundred were injured, and it was all right there for everyone to see . . . for us to see . . . up close and personal in our living rooms.[21]

There's a saying: You can't cure cancer until you know you have it. Well, suddenly "we" had it. It wasn't the kind of awareness people have today . . . and *nothing* remotely like the experience of those actually living it . . . but the shock in Northern living rooms was big enough to register,[22] and in the process, our safe, Democrat world began to tremble. Our identity began to tremble.

"Us." You can't get away from that word and what it means. None of us can, because the definition of "us" is the very issue behind every bit of moral turmoil we've gone through since this nation's beginning. "Us" and its meaning are the core of slavery, racism, homophobia—you name it. "Us," in its better sense, underlay the Revolutionary War, and as the definition began to change and grow, it fostered the Civil War, then the suffragettes and everything FDR accomplished. And that ever-growing definition of "us" underlies our struggle with who we are today as Democrats, every bit of it.

---

21 An effect not unlike us watching the storming of the Capitol Building . . . if we hadn't had four years of Trump to prepare us.

22 To get a real idea of the enormity of what happened, watch the documentary *Eyes on the Prize*.

America was still White when the civil rights movement broke out,[23] but it wasn't the same White Roosevelt grew up in. There was a White middle class now. Suburbs were springing up everywhere,[24] sprawling developments complete with backyards and weekend barbecues and cute little cul-de-sacs . . . safe places, a new kind of normal where people didn't lock their doors till bedtime and children went out to play all by themselves.

Up in the Northern big cities, most of these White suburban families had virtually no contact with anything "Black." Black Americans lived far away in the inner city. Out in the White suburbs, there were no Black neighbors, not in the 1950s. There were no Black kids in the schools. There were no Black parents at PTA meetings, no Black kids on the sports teams, and no Black customers at the supermarket. In these White, Northern suburbs, Blacks weren't looked down upon as much as they weren't looked at at all. Unlike the South, suburban racism up North was half-invisible to White

---

23 According to the US census of 1950, the Northeast was 94.7 percent White. The Midwest and West were above 95 percent. No Brown people to speak of, either. For White supremacists, these were the good old days.

24 More than 1,500,000 new homes were built every year after the war.

people. It was very easy for these suburban dwellers to pretend racism didn't exist at all.[25]

It was extra easy because the ruling word for these new Northern suburbs was "proper." People were polite. They obeyed the rules. They dressed up and went to church. Their children stood respectfully and said the pledge of allegiance in school. And their TV screens . . . the screens that were beginning to alter their lives forever . . . were filled with nice, safe shows like *Ozzie and Harriet* and *Leave It to Beaver*, programs that extolled the safe, orderly suburban way of life.

So it was quite a shock when those same TV screens suddenly blasted out images of snarling mobs trying to attack frightened young Black teenagers in Little Rock, or scenes of enraged, red-faced men dragging peaceful demonstrators off lunch-counter stools and beating them senseless. It was violent and extreme, and, to a lot of those Northern, big-city White suburbanites, deeply disturbing. Nobody was quite ready for a Black family to move in next door, but they couldn't understand why Black Americans in the South had to sit in

---

25 So many Whites today still live in a bubble devoid of the Black American existence, but the "bubble" back then was infinitely greater. There were virtually no Black professional athletes to watch, virtually no Blacks on TV or in the movies, and certainly no documentaries about racism. Alex Haley existed, but *Roots* didn't, and it wouldn't for nearly two more decades.

the back of the bus, why it was such a big deal. Or use separate drinking fountains, or get beat up for wanting to eat lunch at Woolworth's.

But the most disturbing thing for a lot of educated Democrats up North was the idea that the snarling protestors who filled their TV screens, the White faces so filled with hate and violence, looked just like them.

Bogalusa, Louisiana, July 1, 1965.

The Southern segregationists had the same White features. They dressed in the same respectable clothes. The
women carried the same purses, and except for their
expressions of pure hatred, they seemed to act exactly
the same.

By all appearances, they were us, and that jarring idea
forced a lot of Northern Democrats into the beginnings
of some soul-searching, a moral questioning. Certainly
not everybody, as the Republicans were about to prove,
but enough. And the images of snarling dogs and fire-
hoses and burned-out churches kept on coming, horrible images. White faces began to appear among the
demonstrators . . . "us" White faces . . . and some of
them got beat up as well. Some of them died.

Troubled voices began to be heard inside the Democratic Party up North. Maybe people weren't ready for
Black neighbors, but this stuff was something else. This
was violent racism, outright subjugation as a way of life.
Worse, it was almost like "we" were doing it . . . White
people indistinguishable from "us" on the outside were
doing it[26] . . . standing up on TV and saying absolutely
hateful things . . . and taking pride in it.

It was beyond the pale for many, and a reckoning
began. For nearly three decades, we Democrats (we
White Democrats) had coasted along on a moral com-

---

26 Us, it's always about "us."

promise: expressing support for Black Americans while enabling their oppressors. Suddenly, it wasn't so simple anymore. Suddenly, it was political power versus morality, and "we" were going to have to choose. It didn't happen overnight . . . it took a lot more protests and a lot more violence, and the outcome wasn't neat or complete in any sense of the word . . . but social norms began to change, at least about Jim Crow. And so the beginnings of our moral turmoil as a party were born . . . the very one that bedevils us today.

In 1948, some 63 percent of Americans *opposed* integrating the military. By 1964 . . . just sixteen years later . . . 58 percent supported laws to enforce civil rights everywhere.

"We" still preferred to avoid things, of course. Protests made Northern Whites uncomfortable. So did large gatherings of Black Americans. But Jim Crow made us even more uncomfortable, and pressure began to build. It wasn't about "us" yet—Black Americans were still "them"—but the voices that were being raised were definitely speaking about morality, about values, our values as Democrats, and it led to the 1964 Civil Rights Law, the Voting Rights Act of 1965, the Fair Housing Act, and a whole lot more. However limited some of this legislation may seem today, it was huge back then. A side had been chosen, however imperfectly, and the consequences were seismic.

Then Vietnam was dumped on top. A little faraway nothing somehow turned into a bloody, endless war without purpose that was being broadcast into living rooms in full-screen horror, side by side with the civil rights protests. White kids were in the middle of that combat horror as well, their dead bodies lying right alongside the Black kids.

In 1968, it all seemed to come apart. The war in Vietnam imploded, televised across the country in living color. Then Martin Luther King was assassinated, and Robert Kennedy. Rioting broke out, and whole city blocks were burned down while the rest of the nation sat in their living rooms and watched on TV. The Democratic National Convention was engulfed in demonstrations that often verged on rioting. *Star Trek* aired a White man kissing a Black woman, hippies were openly smoking marijuana, and in a few more years, women were burning bras and marching in the streets, lesbians and gays right behind them.

To a lot of people, the country seemed to be coming apart, a vision of slow-motion anarchy that was destroying their very way of life,[27] and it all happened just in time to save the Republican Party.

---

27 If this sounds incredibly familiar, it should.

BIRTH OF THE DEATH STAR

The story of the modern Republican Party is very much a part of our story. In many ways, we're two sides of the American coin; you can't understand one without the other. And like so many other things in all this, the story begins with FDR.

By the time Roosevelt died, he'd turned the GOP into a permanent minority party. The New Deal and its popularity created so much political havoc for the Republicans, and for so long, that they ended up with a major identity crisis after the war. Driven by that, liberal Republicans had risen to the top (yes, liberal Republicans). They were still Big Business all the way . . . small government, fiscal responsibility, the whole nine yards . . . but they were also swimming frantically in the wake of the New Deal, and so they had come up with what might be called "civilized conservatism." No government money to be spent, of course, but they backed a whole raft of do-gooder social ideas in principle. As late as 1960, the Republican national platform supported raising the minimum wage. Yes, it's true. And that same Republican platform also supported extending Social Security, moving forward with school desegregation, and an equal rights amendment for women.[28]

---

28 Hard to believe these days, but it really is true.

These ideas were so liberal, people found it increasingly hard to tell the Republicans apart from the Democrats . . . "Tweedledee and Tweedledum" some called them . . . and that spelled disaster at the polls. Except for Eisenhower (who turned out to be more of a moderate Democrat than a Republican), the Republicans lost . . . a lot.[29]

And we kept on winning. The Democratic way of things was going to go on forever, or so it seemed.

In the early sixties, a band of extreme Republican conservatives stood up and said, "Enough!" These were real ideological firebrands (for the day), no more "fake conservatism" for them. They took over the party, and in 1964, they nominated a candidate who would run on strict conservative ideology. No more pussyfooting around, no more liberal nonsense—this time there'd be a real choice. The candidate's name was Barry Goldwater, and he was a *real* conservative, no doubt about it. His ideology was out there in capital letters, his principles, and he ran on them full steam ahead.

The result of Goldwater's ideological purity? He didn't just lose the election, he was destroyed. The "new" Republicans lost forty-four states, and they lost

---

29 Except for two years under Truman and two under Ike, we controlled the House for thirty-six straight years and the Senate for almost as long.

Barry Goldwater

Barry Goldwater wrote a short book entitled *The Conscience of a Conservative*. It extolled utopian conservatism, a place where the government's only legitimate role was protecting the freedom . . . the absolute freedom . . . of the individual (those individuals who already had freedom, that is). Goldwater argued that allowing the government to do anything more was a sure road to dictatorship . . . especially listening to the popular vote. In his view, letting the will of the people prevail through direct voting led straight to the "tyranny of the masses."[30]

The Conscience of a Conservative became immensely influential among the Republican elite (many of its premises are alive and well today). The book was easy to read, it was stirring in its apparent logic, and it made the stale conservative ideas of the past sound not only exciting, but actually spiritual.[31] Half-hidden in Goldwater's writing was the premise that successful capitalists . . . the wealthy

---

30 A direct quote from his book.

31 "Conservatism therefore looks upon the enhancement of man's spiritual nature as the primary concern"—another direct quote.

class . . . were responsible for the greatness of America, and that maintaining absolute freedom for them and their businesses was essential to the country's continued greatness. And there it was, writ large: the idea that protecting the wealthy was not only proper, it was righteous.

This was truly cunning writing. For the first time since Ayn Rand,[32] it gave utopian conservatism ideological heft, something popular to quote, and Goldwater's book led to an idea that became accepted under Reagan that somehow making insane amounts of money was patriotic, a necessary by-product of the good billionaires do for the country, that billionaires truly are the cream of the crop.

Goldwater's buzzword for all this, his ultimate justification for everything, was "freedom" . . . freedom in the most utopian, simplistic sense possible. At its essence, it was the idea that infringing upon the absolute freedom of the rich in any way gravely endangers everyone else. Which brings us directly to the Republican Party today.[33]

---

32 Ayn Rand was a novelist, best known in the fifties for *The Fountainhead* and *Atlas Shrugged*. She was also an intellectual who set out her own version of bare-bones utopian conservatism which she called objectivism.

33 Which absolutely loves to use that word for just about everything.

the popular vote by more than 22 percent. It was a defeat of epic proportions. Conservatism was dead, or so everyone thought. Then along came Richard Nixon.

Most people remember Nixon for Watergate, but he was actually the beginning of something far more deadly: the Southern strategy. It was just a tactic at the time, but it ultimately led to a new way of thinking about politics that led us straight to Donald Trump.

Quite simply, Nixon's idea was to peel off the Southern White segregationists . . . solid Democrats since the days of the KKK . . . and to do it by skipping everything else (like policy) and appealing directly to their racism.[34] Of course, local Dixiecrat politicians had been doing this since forever, but Republican presidential candidates hadn't. The problem was how. By 1968, enough had changed that presidential candidates couldn't just go around spouting racist language on national TV anymore.

So Nixon and his operatives came up with code words. One of Nixon's political masterminds put it bluntly in an interview: "You start out in 1954 by saying, 'Nigger, nigger, nigger.' By 1968 you can't say 'nigger'—that hurts you, backfires. So you say stuff like forced busing, states' rights, and all that stuff."[35]

---

34 By redefining their sense of "us."

35 Lee Atwater said this out loud in an interview in 1981. Atwater also managed George H. W. Bush's campaign.

It was pure dog whistle, and in an era of forced school desegregation and violent White backlash, it worked like a charm. That was where a lot of Southern White people were at. Nixon as president swept the solid South, even as the Dixie-Democrats kept a firm grip on everything else. And it worked again four years later when he was up for reelection. It worked very well indeed, and GOP operatives noticed something else: it wasn't just pulling in White Southerners, it was attracting White voters in other parts of the country as well. It was grabbing White Democrats as well as Republicans, and this led to a fundamental realization: fear beats ideas. Fear beats everything, a raw emotion that appeals across traditional political groups. What they had was a sure winner, and it required no thinking.

This was truly revolutionary.[36] It meant that from then on, Republican ideology was window dressing, the road to Republican control of government would rest on a message of pure negative emotion. History doesn't run in a straight line. Neither does politics or social change. Cause and effect are often separated in time, and they're messy. Defenders of conservatism will point

---

36 Revolutionary for a modern American political party. Exploiting fear is ageless, the tactic of choice for demagogues and dictators everywhere. To quote Adolf Hitler, "Credibility doesn't matter. The victor will not be asked if he told the truth." A very interesting quote to ponder these days.

to all this messiness as an excuse and say that the ugly things don't represent real conservatism at all. They'll say that today's GOP nastiness is the result of Donald Trump and the likes of Steve Bannon, but the truth is, the nastiness started in 1968, and it's been the driving force behind the GOP ever since . . . something we've chosen to ignore for a very long time.

The Republican operatives of the seventies didn't ignore it, they seized on it, and they made evangelicals their next target. Religious groups in the South had started setting up segregation academies at that point to keep their kids in all-White schools. You couldn't call them "segregation academies" openly, so they were mostly named something akin to "Christian Academy." Religion did play a major role in the curriculum, and pretty soon the original purpose of the schools was all but forgotten, washed away by time and proper messaging, and wishful thinking.

But that original purpose wasn't lost on GOP operatives. As they began to target these religious groups, they realized that Blacks weren't the only ones these groups abhorred. Homosexuals were right up there . . . condemned by the Bible . . . with emancipated women and communism not far behind. And abortion. Abortion was like a nuclear live wire to Southern evangelicals, and the Republicans pounced on it. They pounced on all of it.

In 1972, the Republican national platform still made no reference whatsoever to God or religious issues. By 1980, there was an entire section devoted to abortion, and in 1984, prayer in school and "gratuitous sex" had come on board.

It may be hard for a lot of us to believe, but not so long ago, the Religious Right didn't exist. Churches were just churches, places for faith and devotion, for worshipping God. There was no national political movement involving evangelicals back then, no National Research Council, no Moral Majority. All of that came in the aftermath of the civil rights movement, and an awful lot of it got underway during the presidency of Ronald Reagan.

Ronald Reagan is an icon to Republicans, a virtual saint, but the truth is, he was the real father of the culture wars. He was the man who took our growing Democratic apathy over what was going on in America and stabbed us in the heart with it.

Reagan was an innovator, a man with vision. He saw exactly what was gripping the country and the possibilities it presented, and he set the stage for the Republican comeback with two masterful strokes.

The first was seizing control of language. Reagan saw clearly that if you control the meaning of words, you've won the argument before it starts.[37] And changing the meanings of words was so very easy: just repeat your new meanings over and over and keep doing it until people begin to assume there must be some truth to it. Where there's smoke, there's fire, right?[38]

And Reagan was a professional actor. He had that knowing, grandfatherly way about him. You couldn't not like him, and he knew how to play to the camera. It made him an incredibly effective messenger, and meanings began to change without most people even noticing. "Freedom" and "liberty" slowly became Republican talking points for a lot of Americans. Year by year, people just started accepting it. "Liberal" became a bad word for a lot of people in exactly the same way. So did anything connected to "feminist," and it quickly spread from words to ideas.[39] Ever wonder where the phrase "tax and spend Democrats" came from? Or the commonly held axiom that Democrats are weak on the economy? It certainly didn't come from reality: Reagan

---

37 A fundamental lesson we seem incapable of learning, no matter how many times we're faced with it.

38 This, too, is hardly a new tactic. Goebbels and the Nazis used it to great effect. "Alternative facts" were their entire message, their trademark.

39 Those of you old enough will remember how the American flag came to be associated with Republicans during the Vietnam War, and burning the flag with Democrats, all without anybody noticing what was happening. "USA!" became a GOP chant the same way, and we only started to take it back quite recently with the likes of the Gold Star Khan family at the 2016 convention. The same with patriotism.

drove up the national debt by 186 percent.[40] Every major recession has come under a Republican president, and the only president to balance the budget since World War II was a Democrat (Clinton), but lots of people still believe those axioms. It came from messaging, repeating it over and over and over.

Reagan's second stroke was to implant another revolutionary idea in the public's mind: Government is bad.

This had been the mantra of the billionaires for a long time . . . leave us alone to make money . . . but the postwar liberal Republicans had always considered the idea pretty far out, at least saying it publicly.[41] Reagan made it mainstream. "Government is not the solution to our problem. Government is the problem," is one of his better-known quotes, a message that he repeated endlessly and one that Republican politicians have repeated ever since. This concept is our Prime Directive turned on its head, the ultimate argument against everything Roosevelt stood for, everything we stand for now. Reagan began to speak about it in that gentle, sarcastic way of his, and just like that, the Prime Directive was being questioned. The very role of government was. By 1985,

---

40 This statistic comes from various sources, including thebalance.com. The original data source is the OMB.

41 The very thing that led to Goldwater and *The Conscience of a Conservative*.

50 percent of Americans said they feared big government. By 1994, that number was 64 percent, and now
it's spread to armed militias and QAnon.

To Republican operatives, there was one big moral to
be taken from all this: Fear works. Fear is good.[42] And
the best part is, you don't need facts. You don't need
logic. You don't even need common sense. All you need
is something to fear, emotions to stir up, and endless
repetition . . . as long as the other side (us) doesn't pay
attention.

Reagan did one more thing for the conservative
cause—he gave it a veneer of legitimacy. He took the
ideas of Barry Goldwater that had been so thoroughly
discredited by American voters and repackaged them
as grandfatherly wisdom. He gave them structure and
sound-bite principles, and you just have to admire the
way he did it. "The best minds are not in government. If
any were, business would steal them away," is an excellent example. Coupled with his style and the success of
taking back the Senate for the first time in twenty years,
he became an idol for the Republican Party, a man to be
revered. He set out conservative "principles" and made
them sound respectable. He made standing on those
simple phrases seem reasonable for decades to come.

---

42 To quote Trump's one-time chief strategist, Steve Bannon,
"Darkness is good. Dick Cheney. Darth Vader. Satan. That's power."

OVER THE CLIFF

Once upon a time, we lived in a quaint two-party political system that was easy to understand. There were
Republicans and Democrats, two sides that were easily
defined by the ideas that lay between them. In simple
terms, the Republican Party represented tradition back
then . . . holding on to the past. Our party was about
change, embracing the future. Voters listened, and on
Election Day, they made a choice.

Those days are no more. Traditional politics is gone,
trampled in the dust. What we live in now is a gigantic
clash of two value systems: fear versus ideals.[43] And it's
no accident. Donald Trump was not an accident. Neither was Charlottesville. None of it is. It was developed
by Republican operatives, step-by-step over decades,
right under our noses. They provided the elements of a
master plan; it just needed the right person to put it all
together. And that person arrived in the form of a man
called Newt.

Newt Gingrich. Not the aging presidential wan-
nabe we saw in 2016 or the haggard-looking fellow who
defended Trump after that; we're talking about the original Newt, the young fireball, the shameless self-pro-
moter who bootstrapped his way up on pure chutzpah.

---

43 It's not so simple, but of course, it is.

Gingrich's first step on entering the House of Representatives was to make himself as famous as possible. As he put it, "If you're not in the *Washington Post* every day, you don't exist." As soon as he got a taste of fame, he formed a small group of young, right-wing House members to join him, firebrands who were willing to follow him over the edge.

The Republican establishment was aghast. Even that late in the game, long-term Republicans still approached actual life in Congress with an air of civility. People still cooperated across party lines to get things done.

Newt would have none of it. In his view, modern politics was endless war. You won by destroying your enemy, and his doctrine was simple:

1 – Politics is about power. Governing is irrelevant. Policies and legislation are irrelevant.
2 – You gain power by utterly destroying your opponent. Oppose everything. Cooperation is treason.
3 – The war is won in the media. Attack, attack, attack . . . facts are irrelevant.[44]

Nixon and Reagan paled in comparison to Newt. This was Sherman's March to the Sea, a grand strategy

---

44 This is the real origin of what we know as "alternative facts." The GOP has been using it as a strategy for decades. Trump just proved to be very, very good at it.

that was the real beginning of the culture war.[45] It was nothing short of a plan to obliterate the opposition (us), a literal Death Star Philosophy,[46] and Gingrich showed real genius in carrying it out.

He attacked endlessly, truth be damned, and he attacked on a grand, emotional level.[47] He cast his enemies (us) as epic villains in a great struggle between Good and Evil. In his moral storytelling, we became the devil's messengers, bent on destroying Western civilization.

And he did it with outright character assassination. He took language and labeling to an extreme Reagan never dreamed of. Senior Republicans thought he'd crash and burn, but he didn't care. He was on a mission, and as his fame and influence within the Republican Party grew, his doctrine went from fringe crazy to GOP centerpiece.

Gingrich was also an organizer. He took a minor campaign organization and turned it into a powerhouse to recruit a fresh crop of Republican candidates nation-

---

45 The true beginning of the intense political tribalism that has consumed us in recent years.

46 Any oldsters out there . . . or youngsters . . . who haven't seen the original *Star Wars*, do yourselves a favor and watch it.

47 "I think one of the great problems we have in the Republican Party is that we don't encourage you to be nasty." —Newt, talking to college Republicans

wide, newbies he could inculcate with his doctrine. He created instructional tapes on how to run a campaign and sent them out to anyone even remotely considering running . . . national, state, local level, he didn't care. He wanted it all.

At one point, he created labels for candidates to use on their Democratic opponents, an actual list of attack words that included "sick," "pathetic," "betray," "traitors," and "anti-family." His goal: to have every Republican candidate in the country attack every Democrat with the same words, all the time, everywhere.[48]

It worked. The older smear tactics had won the presidency, but in 1994, Newt watched as "his" Republicans took control of the House of Representatives for the first time in fifty-eight years. It was a very sweet victory, and in short order, he was named Speaker of the House.

Newt burned out rather quickly after that,[49] but his ideas lived on. Rush Limbaugh became number one on talk radio and Fox News was in the wings. Glenn Beck arose, and Laura Ingraham, QAnon yet to come.

And we went on watching.

---

48 There was also a list of good words for Republican candidates to use describing themselves, including "freedom," "common sense," "courage," "family," "prosperity," "vision" . . . and of course . . . "truth."

49 His ego got in the way.

BLOOD IN THE WATER

Newt's newbies thrived in all this, and they multiplied. Over time, this new force of extreme politicians moved on to form groups like the Freedom Caucus. These were the Mark Meadowses and Jim Jordans and Ron DeSantises of the Republican Party, people who would push the culture war to new heights and recruit even more people in their wake. "Oppose everything" became a standard tactic, one that even a seasoned politician like Mitch McConnell would take up.[50]

And it just kept working so well. Pull out the fear at election time, feed the base some red meat, then put the meat away and go about business as usual. The only problem was, the Republicans had to up the ante each time, make the fear just a little bigger. And of course, people started to believe the meat was real. Even a lot of the younger Republican politicians did. Then along came Obama.

This was the literal bogeyman: a Black man with a father from Africa and the middle name of Hussein. The Republicans went at him full throat. The sky was going to fall in if he was elected, the American way of life would end. Cities would burn and we'd be overrun

---

50 "The single most important thing we want to achieve is for President Obama to be a one-term president." —Mitch McConnell

with Brown people. The base ate it up like they had for over a decade. They believed.

But then Obama won, and the sky didn't fall in. Cities didn't burn. None of the predictions happened, and the base got confused. If everything they'd been led to believe was true and the sky hadn't fallen in, then maybe the problem was the Republican Party itself. Maybe it had gotten too cozy in Washington, too comfortable. Maybe it had betrayed them. And so the Tea Party came into being.

Spontaneous or not, the Tea Party was a real movement, a lot more than a bunch of older White folks running around in goofy costumes. It was a radicalized grouping of the most extreme believers in everything the Republican operatives had been putting out for a decade, the literal base, the people who made up all those right-wing rallies and demonstrations. The Tea Party movement was quickly co-opted, *easily* co-opted, but it soon became a question of who had co-opted whom. Red meat became the order of the day—anger at everybody—and a new political phrase appeared: "Getting primaried."[51] The GOP base was up in arms,

---

51 Established Republican politicians in supposedly "safe" seats were suddenly being challenged in the Republican primary by half-unknown upstarts professing to be even more extreme . . . and actually losing to them.

and they weren't going home, not until they saw some change. It was the same fear and anger that had been fostered in them for decades, but now it was out of control, turned against itself. House Majority Leader Eric Cantor, a leading party figure, fell to an upstart right-wing challenger even farther out than he was. Lots of people fell to unknown flamethrowers, and pretty soon, every Republican in Congress was looking over their right shoulder and throwing red meat as fast as they could. Donald Trump's arrival on the scene should have surprised no one, nor his victory.

Us

★

THE COMMON THREAD

A direct moral line passes from the abolitionists who ran the Underground Railroad to our party today. That moral connection, that Common Thread, passes through Harriet Tubman and Sojourner Truth and Abraham Lincoln.[52] It goes through the labor organizing of the late 1800s and the fight against child labor, and Mary Dreier and the garment workers' Uprising of the 20,000. Susan B. Anthony's there. So is Social Security and the electrification of farms and the fight over voting rights. So are LBJ's Great Society and Obamacare, and every bit of economic, social, and political activism in between.

The Common Thread is that natural human impulse toward fairness, the impulse toward justice in the deepest sense of the word. It's that part of people throughout history that has clung to the idea of the golden rule. That impulse has been overwhelmed for much of his-

---

52 Oh, yes, Honest Abe is one of us. He'd roll over in his grave at being labeled a Republican today.

tory by our tendency toward greed and violence, by our hatred and intolerance and fear, but the existence of that Common Thread as a part of our soul is why slavery no longer exists in the world. It's why democracy does exist, as imperfect as it may be.

Our adherence to the Common Thread as modern Democrats hasn't always been a straight line and it hasn't always been a solid line . . . and it's often been incredibly weak . . . but it's always been there, somewhere. Everything that has pushed us forward as a party since 1933 . . . truly forward morally . . . has had its origins in the Common Thread, in America's centuries-long fight against injustice and inequality and the lack of opportunity. That singular Common Thread . . . not just the drive, but the results that were eventually accomplished . . . is the origin of the Prime Directive. It's the essence of why we're a party, and we should be proud of it.

But as a party, we've lost our grip on that thread in recent years. We talk the talk . . . we keep coming up with all sorts of policies and positions . . . but we've slowly stopped walking the walk. We've begun to drift as a party. We've become complacent, arrogant, and more than a little elitist . . . and in the process, we've lost touch with our base, which means we've lost touch with who we are.

A lot of us are too young to remember, but we were the dominant party . . . the national power . . . for virtually fifty years. Think about that. Five straight decades

of winning election after election, virtually uninter-
rupted control of both houses of Congress,[53] and that
control ran right through all the turmoil of the sixties
and early seventies. It ran through Nixon's Southern
strategy. It ran through Reagan and the first stirrings of
the cultural revolution, and it was still going strong in
1990. We just kept winning, and it was Roosevelt's legacy that did it: a grand coalition based above all on labor
and farmers and Black Americans.[54] Keep 'em happy,
and they keep us in power. It was a formula that just
worked so well, and no matter what adjustments we had
to make, we clung to that idea like mother's milk. Never
mind what the Republicans were up to, never mind that
we saw exactly what they were doing. We were still winning, so we leaned back and smirked and went on doing
exactly the same old stuff. And it was easy, because by
then, we had a lot of the same old people doing it.

Representative John Dingell served in the House for
fifty-nine years. Six whole decades. That's longer than
most of us have been alive. John Conyers served for
fifty-two, and good old Emanuel Celler managed forty-
nine. Twenty-eight politicians have served in the House

---

53 Except for those two years under Eisenhower
and two under Truman.

54 Adjustments were made, of course—adding groups, changing
the pitch—but it was always identity politics at its core.

of Representatives for forty years or more during the modern era. Twenty-four of those are Democrats. Only four are "recent" (since 1970).[55]

The point is not whether these were good people or whether they were good at their jobs. The point is, staying in office *became* their job. Staying in office became their career, and it was all based on using the same old way of thinking, over and over again.[56] It made coasting on the grand coalition a way of life, an arrogance so deep it was hardly even visible.[57] That arrogance, that complacent belief that nothing had to change, led us blind through the massive social changes of the seventies and eighties,[58] a period when the country was begging for new leadership, a new way of thinking. So

---

55 Starting dates for some of the others in the longevity legion: 1941, 1939, 1935, 1928, 1914, and my favorite, Robert Doughton, who was first elected in 1911. Doughton served through Presidents Taft, Wilson, Harding, Coolidge, Hoover, Roosevelt, and Truman. He was probably eying Eisenhower, but he died in 1954 at age ninety.

56 Thinking that included entrenched local machine politics and Democratic "clubs," shadowy organizations that came to basically run a lot of big-city politics.

57 As much as we talked about equality back then, all our national candidates (except Geraldine Ferraro for vice president) were White men right up to 2008, and up until 2011, the chairman of the Democratic National Committee was essentially the same.

58 Not everyone in the party, for sure, but it was true of the establishment and the leadership, those that set our course.

Reagan stepped into the void and filled it with his carefully crafted charisma, slowly turning voters Republican with his skillful ways while we just smiled and watched. Complacency and arrogance are the eternal price of one-party dominance, and we paid for it dearly.

That same complacency and arrogance also fed our peculiarly Democratic affliction of Good Guy-itis. FDR was practically a saint by the end of his life, our national savior. He put working people first, and there was not an ounce of doubt about who the good guys were when he died, about who was fighting for the right things. We were. And we went on being the good guys right through the 1950s. We were champions of the workingman, the factory worker, the unions. Nobody ever doubted who we were, not even the Republicans. It never had to be explained or defended, people just knew, and somehow that enormous assumption has worked its way into our DNA. No matter what's happened, no matter how many decades of enormous change have taken place, no matter how effectively the Republicans have labeled us in a different light, we just go on with this incredibly smug belief that somehow, everyone knows we're the good guys. That it's obvious. That we don't have to explain it. It's another form of complacency, and as we've drifted farther and farther from our base and closer and closer to becoming "the Establishment," it's left us obsessed with proper policies and talking points and tests of moral purity that only the coastal elite are really in touch with. That kind of thinking carried us right through 2016 and Hillary Clinton's devastating defeat.

We like to point out all the mistakes Clinton made as a candidate . . . if she'd only done this or she'd only done that . . . but the truth is, it shouldn't have mattered. The truth is an awful lot of Americans were just fed up with things. People don't always know what's right, but they often know when something's wrong. By 2016, an awful lot of people knew something was wrong, and it wasn't just Black Americans. Entire ways of life were disappearing with no end in sight . . . incomes, jobs, whole towns gone with no real explanation, no sense of how to change it . . . no sense of how *we* were going to change it. An awful lot of people wanted a better way. They didn't know what, but they wanted a change, just like they had back in Roosevelt's day. They wanted someone to have a vision.

Trump didn't win over all those wavering Democrats and independents because of what he stood for. Clinton lost them because of what she didn't stand for. We lost them. Above everything else, 2016 was about a final failure, not just of our way of thinking but of our sense of who we are.[59] What we face today . . . what 2020 made

---

59 There are those who cling to the idea that she won the popular vote. The truth is, she won the popular vote against a man who many people thought was a despicable human being, and she lost the House as well.

abundantly clear[60] . . . is that this is nothing less than the search for our identity, something we haven't really been sure of since the New Deal. That search, that hunger, is exactly what was behind Bernie Sanders's incredible rise. That same hunger, that same confusion about who we are . . . what and who we stand for . . . is why we had twenty-five candidates in the 2020 Democratic presidential primary, and it's exactly why Biden ended up as our candidate . . . the only compromise possible.

EMOTION VERSUS REASON

The elite of our party are forever trying to be enlightened, to couch our messages in intellectual ideas, to "resurrect the primacy of reason over passion" as one scholar put it.[61] This amounts to fighting a new war with the already-failed weapons of the old. It's the French standing behind the Maginot Line all over again,[62] and it leaves us endlessly having to explain and defend.

---

60 Don't focus on Biden's victory, focus on the blue wave that didn't happen. Focus on the idea that against someone like Donald Trump, Biden only got 51 percent of the popular vote. That 51 percent is important.

61 Jeffrey Rosen, president of the National Constitution Center, via the *Atlantic*.

62 A nice little history lesson if you're new to it. Look it up.

Modern politics isn't about facts. It isn't about logic, and it isn't about policies or positions. It's about emotional perception. People don't vote on ideas, they vote on emotion. All people do, you and me included. However much we like to think we're driven by our ideas and our thinking, what makes us argue, what makes us want to pull our hair out at times, is the emotion we've attached to our logic. And it's emotion that drives us to the polls and "pulls that lever." FDR understood that. It was in every speech he gave, and it's why people wept when he passed away. It's only us modern Democrats who seem to balk at the idea.

Being driven by emotions is not a bad thing, it's just human. What makes it good or bad is what the emotions are tied to, what needs and values . . . and facts . . . are used to inspire them. FDR understood that as well. It's why hope and optimism and courage are what he is remembered for, as much as the very real results he accomplished, because he used those emotions so skillfully.

There's another thing we always seem to ignore, and it's huge: **The vast majority of Americans don't have time in their lives to follow politics closely**. That goes for Democrats as well as Republicans, and it goes double for policy debates about complex issues.[63] Working people don't care about Medicare for All versus Obamacare. They just want affordable health care. **They want to**

be able to trust someone to take care of it for them, that's what their vote is about. And that's exactly how Trump snuck in.[64]

Elections are all about the emotional perception of who we are. It was true in Roosevelt's day and it's true a thousand times more since the Gingrich revolution and the advent of social media and cable news. Winning is about messaging emotion, a lesson the Republicans have become masters at while we've mostly stood around and watched.[65]

Modern Republicans view messaging as the end-all, a route to power that is disconnected from truth. It's messaging without morals, and it's what led directly to Donald Trump and the mess he created.

We *are* moral. We do have a Common Thread, and so our messaging needs to be tied to our values. It has to spring from our core beliefs and the issues that spring

---

63 There is no such thing as a perfect policy. No matter how well you think it out, any policy is open to attack, which is why we spend so much time defending ourselves instead of going after the Republicans on the underlying values.

64 "Only I can fix it" may be the most effective of all the outrageous promises he made.

65 Bernie Sanders being a clear exception. He didn't inspire his followers because of Medicare for All. What drove those enormous turnouts was his emotional appeal, his basic beliefs and the way he expressed them.

from them in turn, and that's good news because **those core beliefs excite people**. Equal rights for women excites people. So does a living minimum wage and clean air (to say nothing of clean water). Affordable health insurance for everyone won us the House in 2018, and an end to racism has become a value that drives millions of people. These are values and basic issues you don't have to explain. You only have to put them out there properly, lead with them . . . and let the Republicans do the defending.

THE END OF NORMAN ROCKWELL

Roosevelt's world is gone. We're no longer a nation of quaint small towns or a mighty force of middle-class factory workers, the kind Rockwell immortalized in his paintings. Those things still exist, but not for most of us. We live in gigantic suburbs now, or cities. We're a population where 90 percent of us have a high school education, a third have some form of college,[66] and we're no longer "White." Like it or not, change began to grip this nation the day the civil rights movement broke out in the fifties. Vietnam, economics, and technology propelled it forward right through the nineties, decades that left huge change in their wake.

---

66 US Census, 2010.

A FEW WORDS ABOUT

Elitism

We recoil at the idea of being called elitist, of being snobs, all of us do. We stand for the people. Bettering people's way of life is our Prime Directive. The Common Thread is real and our policies back it up, so how can we be elitist?

Attitude, that's how. And language. As long as a big part of this country feels that "we" are talking down to "them" . . . that we're not listening . . . then we have a problem. And as a party, we are guilty. Whether we realize it or not, so many of our activists and spokespeople are guilty of shoving elitist standards and politically correct language on everyone else, an endless quest for intellectual, moral purity that turns off a lot of people.

Be clear: this is NOT about the issues. This is not about one single one of the very real injustices plaguing this country, and it's not about any of the ideas that have been set out to fix those injustices. It's not about activism. It's not about progressivism, or ending racism, or establishing universal health care, or the validity of alternate lifestyles. It's about the way all that is presented. It's about the messaging, and the messaging is all about the mindset of the people presenting those messages.

We started out as the party of working folks, blue-collar, and we still like to see ourselves that way, only a little more universal. The truth is, we're primarily urban-based, with a heavy emphasis on "Black" and "educated." That's where our core voters are. It's also where the Democrat establishment is, in major coastal big cities like New York and Boston and Los Angeles, but especially in Washington. That's where the power is, and that's where the intellectual activism resides, the forces that together shape our thinking and messaging as a party. And that world is elite.

And so elitism will always creep into our messaging. It's inevitable, and that's why having our core values stated in basic terms is so important. It forces us back to the real issues. And that's why *we* are so important . . . you and me . . . the ordinary people who make up the party. We're the only ones who can temper things over time. We're the only ones who can make sure common sense and basic values are always at the center of things. We're the only ones who can pressure the elite and pull our messaging back to where it belongs, messaging that connects. And if we don't message in a way that can connect with everyone . . . connect with the very people we seem to disagree with . . . we will never convince them. And if we don't convince, we lose.

Take a moment to think about it. Back in the 1960s, a woman needed a man to sponsor her in order to get a credit card.[67] Yep, that's right, you needed your husband's approval (or your father's, or even your brother's). It was extremely difficult for a woman to become a doctor or a lawyer because medical schools and law schools didn't want them.[68] Prior to 1960, no woman was allowed to run a race in the Olympics that was longer than two hundred meters because it was considered "too strenuous."[69]

Thirty years later, 40,000 women soldiers charged into the Middle East during Desert Storm.[70] More than 40 percent of law students were women, and Madeleine Albright became secretary of state. Ruth Bader Ginsburg was named a Supreme Court justice, and women

---

67 Credit cards among other things. In 1960, marital rape didn't exist. A husband couldn't rape his wife because a wife was legally required to submit to her husband. By definition, she couldn't be raped. It wasn't any easier if you were gay. Sex between gay men was a felony in every state in the country in 1960, punishable by a lengthy term of imprisonment and/or hard labor. Something to remember when people talk about "the good old days."

68 When Ruth Bader Ginsburg entered Harvard Law School in 1956, she and the other eight women faced five hundred men.

69 It was 1984 before the women's marathon was added as an event.

70 Five years later, a woman flew a jet in combat. In 2005, Sergeant Leigh Ann Hester won the Silver Star for valor in combat.

began to head major corporations.[71] But as huge as all that is, those years are nothing compared to what has been going on recently.

Do you remember the slogan for the original iPhone: "This changes everything"? It easily describes what the computer has done to the entire world we live in. Smartphones have been around less than fifteen years.[72] Fifteen years. That's less time than it took for you to graduate from high school and we've gone from looking things up in the library to having unlimited information in our pocket. The ability to stand in front of the Eiffel Tower in Paris, take a picture and send it to your friend in Omaha, and talk to her at the same time . . . that's all new. Nobody could do that twenty years ago. Most people couldn't even imagine it. Facebook is new, too, and Twitter and chat groups and TikTok and whatever other apps have come along while you've been reading this. It's the ability to connect with people all over the world, to talk to people you've never met personally and share ideas with them, to find like-minded peo-

---

71 Jump to today for a sense of the enormity of the change: women CEOs head General Motors, UPS, Oracle, and General Dynamics among others. See *Forbes* for a full list.

72 Way back in . . . 2007. And the internet hasn't been around a whole lot longer. In 1995, 14 percent of the country had internet access (dial-up!). By the year 2000, that number was 50 percent. Today, it's nearly everybody.

ple all over the place. All that has changed social norms forever, and . . . grubby as it may seem . . . social norms rule politics.

Social norms are society's guidelines, the guardrails of what we accept as right and wrong.[73] And so these same social norms are the guidelines . . . and limitations . . . for politics. Always and forever. Slavery was morally wrong in 1761,[74] but it was only a hundred years later that social norms had changed enough to cause the Civil War. Racial inequality was wrong in 1861, but it's only today that we're really beginning to face up to it.

Quite simply, social norms set the rules. Individuals often transcend social norms, of course. We tend to call them "ahead of their time" (or "heretics"), but national culture never transcends the norms of the moment. It's the very definition of "norm."

"Politics is the art of the possible"[75] is an apt quote, and it describes the relationship between social norms and politics exactly. It is a precise explanation of why the New Deal, JFK's New Frontier, and LBJ's Great Society

---

73 Altering these norms, setting them back, is one of the most dangerous things Trump has done.

74 It was wrong back when Spartacus was alive, too. People just didn't think it was.

75 A quote from Otto von Bismarck, ironically. The full quote: "Politics is the art of the possible, the attainable—the art of the next best."

went as far as they did, pushing the envelope to the limit, but going no farther.

"Possible" is a word to remember as we struggle with who we are. **You don't become the majority party by being ahead of your time, you do it by being in your time**. And that's what makes now so special, so truly historic, because what's "possible" now is changing in a way that has never been seen before. Up until now, our Common Thread . . . the moral impulse that has steadily grown inside us . . . has never had free rein. The values we seek out intuitively, the truths we see on the horizon—those have forever been bumping up against the social norms of the day. As Democrats, we have always faced limitations on our morality, to what we can change, to what we can even propose . . . but all that is disappearing, fast.

In 1995, just 48 percent of Americans approved of interracial marriage. By 2004, 76 percent approved. In 2008, a Black man was elected president of the United States, and in 2020, Black Lives Matter broke out . . . and most of the demonstrators were White.[76]

In 1996, 73 percent of the country was against gay marriage. Eight years later, the first state legalized it. By 2014, thirty-five states had. That's a span of just eighteen years.

---

76 See Notes for some really interesting stats, including how many outsiders (how few) were involved in the big marches.

In 1980, this country was still 83 percent White. Today, we're barely more than 60 percent White, and the change is evident everywhere. Television features Asian faces now, and Black faces and Hispanic faces and Indian faces . . . and most significantly of all, nobody even notices anymore. Diversity is a new norm for us, supported by a growing majority of Americans.[77] Like it or not, diversity has become a part of who we are now, of who we are as a nation.

All this, everything that's happened, is more than a staggering amount of social change. It amounts to a seismic shift in fundamental attitudes. For the very first time in American history, a critical mass of this country is beginning to look at what equal rights and equal opportunity really mean, for everyone. It's new, it's teetering . . . it's definitely not firmly established yet . . . but it's there. That's good. That's more than good, it's exciting. But it carries a dark side as well.

A lot of people are confused. The old values seem to be gone and there's nothing clear to replace them, just the promise of even more change, and it leaves people vulnerable to demagoguery. It leaves them susceptible to wild conspiracy theories and ultrapartisan personalities. On top of that, cable news is blasting away twenty-four hours a day and no one but a dedicated news junky

---

77 PEW, Quinnipiac, PRRI . . .

can keep up with it. It's no wonder people are confused. They're more than confused. They're disturbed, fearful on a visceral level.

And that's why we need a voice. Americans need a voice, a true north to guide by, and we need it now . . . something that isn't spin, something that cuts through all the political and cultural noise and says it's genuine.[78] We are looking for a political moral compass to guide us, and there is only one North Star in the sky. There is only one thing that will endure down the very long road that lies ahead: our core values, and the basic beliefs they inspire.

BACK TO THE BEGINNING

"Life, Liberty, and the Pursuit of Happiness" are not randomly chosen words. Along with "all men are created equal," they are the very genesis of our country. The Constitution is our how-to guide, our operating manual, but the opening of the Declaration of Independence is our soul. It's a declaration of our very motivation to form a country, words that everyone turns to, and it's an excellent place for us to start.

---

78 Taking advantage of this hunger is exactly how Donald Trump won the presidency. The fact that he lied about everything and was morally repugnant to boot just points to how desperate a lot of voters were for a voice.

In modern English, "Life, Liberty, and the Pursuit of Happiness" mean "Justice, Freedom, and Opportunity."

Justice means much more than racial justice or legal justice; it means a just society. It means a nation where everyone's worth as a human being is respected, a country where every single citizen is safe in their person, their house, and their family . . . regardless of race, creed, gender, economic status, or anything else. Every single person.

Freedom . . . democracy . . . means safe, free elections, where every citizen (yes, every single citizen) enjoys full access to voting rights, and where elections are guaranteed against fraud, manipulation, or corruption of any kind. And it means those guarantees are transparent, where every citizen of any political persuasion can readily see the fairness of the process itself, should it be at the local, state, or national level . . . for there can be no fair elections unless everybody respects the institutions that produce them. Freedom means a lot more than that, but without democracy, it means nothing at all.

And finally, we have opportunity, and that's a big one. Opportunity means exactly that: a fair chance. It does not mean a guarantee of success, or an equal standard of living. In fact, it means just the opposite. It means our innate qualities as human beings should determine what we become, not the accident of our birth, nor the privilege of our parents, nor the limitations of our neighborhood. And *that* means a great deal. It means putting education first, ahead of tanks and corporate handouts and pork barrel projects—everything special interests spend millions promoting. Putting education first . . . and education for the underprivileged first of the first . . . is something we've never done since the colonial days in New England. We talk forever about our respect for education, but in a country where everything is measured in dollars, it's easy to see what the real priorities are.

Equal opportunity also means universal access to acceptable medical care. Without that, no one has equal opportunity in anything.

It also means access to a decent job, a way to work and support yourself and your family, no matter the accident of your birth. And that right applies to disenfranchised factory workers and coal miners facing unemployment just as much as it does to poverty-stricken people in inner cities. It means everyone, regardless of political party.

And of course it means an end to racism, of any sort, against any group. It means an end to all of the above and a heck of a lot more, and that's the beauty of the word.

But we're going to have to declare more than that, because we're going to have to deal with the role of government, the very foundation of everything Roosevelt stood for, the basis for everything we've accomplished. The Republicans and their benefactors have attacked that role for a long, long time, and so we have to declare it as well.

Which raises even more questions. Do we touch on family values? Or patriotism? The Bill of Rights? And how do we do all that in a simple form that is easy to read, emotionally compelling, and that will be just as true twenty years from now as it is today?[79]

One thing is certain: **Our declaration of values has to be devoid of politics, especially our own**. Our core values and beliefs need to rise above all that. People . . . all people, even those who oppose us . . . need to know in their heart that the values we set out are true. They need to sense these are American values. Above all, they need to see them as basic goals, things we intend to accomplish—not the way we plan to do it—and that means there is no room for ideology.

Ideology is very tempting. Some of us have toyed with it from time to time . . . and rather recently . . . but the truth is, the Democratic Party has never had an ideology.[80] We've had plenty of policies. We've had plenty of programs and approaches, but we've never set out an

---

79 And that's really important. There's a very long road ahead of us, and nobody . . . absolutely nobody . . . knows what twists and turns are coming.

80 Party platforms? White papers? Sure. But a true doctrine, a set of basic principles to govern all this? Not at all.

ideology. We've never written one down. We've never even enunciated one, and there's a reason for that.

Despite all our activism, despite our idealistic fervor and tangents of the moment, we're a party of pragmatists. We're about helping everyday Americans and doing it with whatever works. Roosevelt was the original pragmatist, the original nonideologue, and he laid down a marker that has served the country well. Pragmatism, getting things done, is what most Americans still believe in.

As Democrats, we have always been open to any real approach that solves problems, most definitely including using the private sector (something we need to be very clear about . . . especially to ourselves).[81] If we've often had a heavier emphasis on government intervention, it's often because of the enormous abuses that the Republicans and their billionaire allies have snuck into the economic system and the damage they've done to the country in the process. The truth is, we *are* the original dealmakers. Roosevelt passed the New Deal in the face of intense political opposition. LBJ passed his groundbreaking civil rights legislation in spite of the Dixiecrats and wholesale national racism. And these

---

81 Ideas like "revolution" and "socialism" may sound good to some people in the passion of the moment, but they are never . . . ever . . . going to be embraced by the general public. Major reform is a very different story . . . and it requires very different wording.

are just a few examples. We are the real dealmakers . . . the real authors of progress . . . and we've got the goods to prove it. The Republicans don't, we do. But we've let the American public lose sight of that . . . we've let the Republicans make the public lose sight of it. It's our own damn fault, and it's time to fix it. It's time to put our divisions behind us, to put our arguments in their proper place, between ourselves. **It's time for us to reconnect emotionally with the American public, all of us, together**.

Our party has always been divided between moderates and progressives . . . the realists and the idealists, the FDRs and the Eleanors, the establishment that worries about elections and getting things done and the activists who care about what should be done. We always will be. We will always be arguing over these things,[82] but it's a false choice to think we need to *be* one or the other. We need to be "us." That's what all this is about, everything we're struggling over: our sense of identity.

Forget about elections for the moment. Forget about political campaigns and policies. That is a different discussion . . . a very important one, but very, very different. This is about the way the American people perceive us as a party, their gut sense of who we are. That identity . . . and the one the Republicans have claimed for

---

82 Especially during primaries, every single time.

their own . . . is precisely how this country gets divided into warring camps. Identity is what drives the political and cultural polarization that has become the center of politics today, and that's what we have to change.

Establishing our real sense of identity with the American public . . . then expanding it to more and more people . . . is exactly how we become the true majority party. That means our basic identity as a party can't be about Midwestern values versus the big city, or jobs versus civil rights—not anymore. It has to be about us, our basic beliefs and how we present them, the very image we set before the American people. **This is all about values, and it has been since 1933.**

RACE

Race holds a very special role for us. In many ways, the issue of race and Black Americans has all but defined our moral struggle as Democrats. It's a battle we've waged with ourselves for more than seven decades, and we still haven't figured it out.[83]

We did have it figured out back in 1933. It was easy . . . "we" were White. No doubt about it back then. We were married to the Dixiecrats, with one foot still

---

83 Progress? Sure. Something we as Democrats
have figured out? Absolutely not.

stuck in our racist past, and our grasp on the Common Thread and race was extremely weak.[84] There was Eleanor's voice, and a few others, but they often echoed in silence. Back in those days, Black Americans were definitely not "us." They were an adjunct, a group that followed in our (White) shadow, hoping for protection. We gave it in little drips and drabs, and that was the beginning of identity politics.

We Democrats were still White when Black Americans began to stand up and demand their rights. We were White when their demands got louder and we were forced to begin coming to terms with what the Common Thread really meant. "We" were still White decades later, when we all but depended on the Black American vote yet had only begun to embrace a few White women in positions of power.

Well, we are White no more. The last two decades have ended that. But we're not Black either. And we're not Hispanic or Asian American. The truth is, as Democrats, we no longer have a clear racial identity, and it's the cause of a lot of our current turmoil. No one quite knows what's going on, let alone what's coming down the pike. Who, exactly, are we going to be in five years? In ten

---

84 And not just about Black Americans. We are, after all, the party that interned Japanese Americans and turned away Jewish refugees during World War II.

years? In twenty? And how are we going to get there? Are we going to wander forward, pushed around by events, always reacting, or are we going to choose our path?

Politics can't answer this kind of question. Election campaigns and the struggle of day-to-day events are terribly important, but they're about the present, what needs to be done right now. This question is about our long-term future. It demands perspective, and the hardest part of finding that perspective is getting past the one thing that affects each and every one of us—that persistent heritage we carry of being a White party. You may think it's obvious, that it's easy to point out, easy to try and change. But an awful lot of what our White heritage has done to us is subconscious. It's unseen baggage that we carry around without even realizing it. All of us do, Black and White, Native American and everyone else, assumptions and biases and knee-jerk emotional reactions that are embedded so deeply inside us, we take them for unspoken truths. And that White heritage is going to go on confusing us for quite a while because we're not going to be who we're truly becoming racially for a long time yet. And so we're not going to have a clear vision of what that really means for just as long . . . but we need to start thinking about it. We need to start talking.

One thing's for sure: if we really want to be the party of everybody, our central message going forward can't be about racial identity. If the Democratic Party truly is everyone . . . if we're Black as well as White, Hispanic, and everything else . . . then we cannot separate out one group from ourselves and say they're different, even in their time of need.[85] And our basic message . . . our core values . . . can't seem to be coming from just one group.[86] However difficult it may be, whatever we have to say down the road has to roll off Black lips just as easily and fully as White, be just as universal in application and just as convincing. Hispanic voices have to be just as comfortable with it, and so do Asian Americans. **Our central message has to be coming from all of us, and it has to be about all of us**.

And yet, racism against Black Americans stands apart. It just does. It's persisted for more than two hundred years, a stain on our country that has thwarted endless attempts to eliminate it, and now it's growing into a force that threatens to convulse the nation. It cannot be denied, and there's a reason for that.

America has faced two forms of racial discrimination. One kind is displayed against immigrants. That discrimination (racism when it's extreme) is based on a

---

85 How do you talk about the plight of Black Americans without making them "them"?

86 Be it anger or defensiveness, action or reaction, subconsciously our messaging so often seems to come from being White. Or Black.

very human bias against outsiders, an innate prejudice against people who look differently, speak differently, or act differently. It's been going on since the beginning of time, and it isn't racial at its core, it's cultural.[87] And when immigrant groups change their culture . . . over generations . . . that discrimination slowly ends. The descendants of those immigrants become part of the culture that initially rejected them. They assimilate. Over time, they become part of the greater whole.[88]

Racism against Black Americans is different. It's founded on the idea that Black people are subhuman. It shouldn't surprise anyone that such an idea sprang up in America, the institution of plantation slavery demanded it. How else do you justify treating people like animals? How else do you rationalize owning slaves with being a Christian (and a supporter of freedom)? As time went by, a whole culture was created around this idea of Black subhumanity, a complete Southern society with far-reaching rules of behavior that included institutional violence. Racial "theories" were developed to legitimize it all, theories of White racial superiority that

---

87 Sorry, but the Irish in Northern Ireland didn't fight a terrorist war against each other because they were of different races. Neither did the people of former Yugoslavia. Language, religion, manner of dress, local customs, and taboos . . . all of that is cultural.

88 Discrimination . . . often violent . . . against Irish and Italians was once common. Now it's little more than a historical footnote.

went on being expounded as "scientific" right up to Hitler and the Final Solution.[89]

Not every White American felt that way back then,[90] but it's no accident that by the time the North went to war to end slavery, giving those freed slaves actual equality was not popular at all ("Black *American*" wasn't even a term people used). Sending "them" back to Africa was popular. Abraham Lincoln himself spoke of "your race" and "ours" and the need for "separation."[91] Being anti-slavery in those days definitely didn't mean you were anti-racism.

Way before Lincoln, the idea that Black Americans were somehow less than fully human was buried deep in the subconscious of most White people. Few wanted to talk about it, but that incredible bias was there, and it has lingered in one form or another for a long, long time. It's where Jim Crow came from, and lynching, and the opposition to desegregation and voting rights, all the way down to the visceral hatred of Obama more than a few Whites still hold on to. Changes have hap-

---

89 And can still be found.

90 All White Americans have never been of one voice about anything. They definitely aren't now.

91 The dismissiveness is inherent in the labels that were used for so long (and often still are) . . . "colored," "negroes," "Blacks." Those who are White never refer to themselves as "Whites"; they say, "White people."

pened, a lot of changes, but it's only during the past cou-
ple of decades that large numbers of White people . . .
large numbers of Democrats . . . are actually beginning
to look at what this really is all about. And that brings
us back to the question that underlies this entire book:
who are "we"?

It's difficult to answer. Even writing about it is. Finding words for the Black experience or the White experience in this book was hard enough. Writing those words
as "us" . . . all of us . . . required constant rewriting and
endless outside criticism, and even then it's flawed. The
truth is, trying to grasp the idea of "us" with any real
perspective means stepping outside of the anger and
guilt and frustration and ignorance that, one way or
the other, affects every single one of us. To truly step
outside all that is virtually impossible, and yet that is
exactly what we need to do . . . somehow . . . if we truly
want to become the party of everybody.

How, then, do we reconcile our very different attitudes
on race? And, yes, they are different because *we* are different . . . those of us who make up the Democratic Party . . .
and we always will be, and that carries enormous impli-
cations. If you're not Black, you can look at racism[92] as a
huge issue, a terrible injustice. You can go out and march
after watching horrible events on TV, but it's still just

---

92 Against Black Americans.

an issue. So is climate change, or gay rights, or election reform. If you're Black, it isn't an issue, it's your life. It's something that affects you deeply every single day, something that's terribly personal in terms of anger and frustration. Those of "us" who aren't Black can walk away from a march and turn to something else. Those of us who are Black can't, and that is never going to change.

And what about the racial issues facing Native Americans? Or Hispanic Americans? Or Asian Americans? Everyone's racial issues are important to them. And every injustice is valid.[93] And if that wasn't enough, we all have differing ideas of what's actually going on, even of what the basic facts are.[94]

So how do we do it? How do we turn all those differences and conflicts into a "we"? How are we going to deal with all the other nonracial injustices and issues at the same time? And how on earth are we going to do it with one voice?

There is no simple answer, and there's not going to be one for years. But there's not going to be any answer at all if we don't start talking about it, really talking about it . . . and not just to the people who look and think like

---

93 Not recognizing that validity is as big a mistake as not recognizing the urgency of racism against Black Americans.

94 And we're not talking about "MAGA distortion." We're talking about reading and viewing and experiencing slightly different things . . . what that does to our perspective and our conversations.

we do. We need to start talking to all the people who don't look and sound like us. We need to find a way.

The only possible place to begin is with our basic beliefs, our core values, the ideas we hold that are bigger than policies, bigger even than issues. We need to be discussing these ideas, arguing about them until we have consensus, then putting them at the forefront of everything we do. And our messaging needs to be about these things as well, especially on racism. Setting our house in order on race is *not* about messaging.[95] But winning elections is. Successful politics is . . . especially regarding race . . . and getting us beyond "51 percent" definitely is. And that's why the words that we repeat over and over to the rest of the country have to begin with the idea that racial injustice in any form whatsoever is un-American, a violation of the very Declaration of Independence that founded this country. That's what we have to keep hammering away at, injustice . . . racial injustice when it's about race, but any injustice when it's appropriate . . . economic injustice in rural America, the cultural injustice of entire, mostly White communities being left behind, or any of the other, ever-changing issues that confront us. That is our true message, the one that promises to make us whole: our goal is to make America a truly just society, once and for all, for everybody.

---

95 Quite the opposite.

Them

"Know thy enemy. . ."[96]

★

WHO ARE THESE PEOPLE ANYWAY?

Have you ever wondered why the Republican Party has spent so much time and energy doing bad things to their own voters? Most of the GOP's base . . . the ones that fill the rallies and hold up signs at demonstrations . . . are middle-class, and a lot of them are working-class. Regardless of whether they're "getting by" or really struggling, all of them need health insurance. So why has the Republican Party opposed giving it to them? And not just opposed it, but fought it tooth and nail, tried to beat the thing to death? What about clean air? Why have the Republicans stood against that? All of their supporters breathe. Why have the Republicans stood against action on clean drinking water and decontaminated soil? Why have they opposed the Bureau of Consumer Protection and all the other things that would so obviously have made their own supporters' lives bet-

96 Sun Tzu, a very long time ago.

ter? And the Republicans certainly could've stood up for these things. They could've come up with their own solutions, or even taken ours and labeled them conservative, then taken credit for it (putting us in even more serious trouble). But they didn't. They still don't. Why? What possible reason could they have?

Republican politicians love the appearance of ideology. They love to dress things up in doctrine to justify what they're doing. They love lofty-sounding political slogans, the same political euphemisms Reagan was so good at creating. And like Karl Marx before them[97] (and Newt), they love to project this ideology as a grand battle between two moral systems, Good versus Evil—the idea that we are a country that has lost its way, an "America in peril," a place where moral values are in endless decay because of the terrible spread of "socialism."[98] Most of all, they love to invoke "conservative principles." Those words get repeated over and over, a kind of political Ten Commandments, the one answer to moral decay, the one thing that can save Western Civilization.

So, what are these conservative principles? What do they mean specifically? For that matter, what is a conservative? Surely it's written down for all to see. Surely there's a central tenet in black and white?

---

97 Oh, yes, irony.

98 It used to be communism, but that became a little stale.

Well, there are actually two sets of conservative principles. There's what their supporters . . . "the base" . . . believe, and then there's what the Republicans themselves believe. It's not the same thing at all.

For supporters, we can turn to the dictionary:[99]

Conservative: a person who is averse to change and holds to traditional values and attitudes.

It's a basic definition of being socially conservative, and that is the beating heart of a huge swath of Republican voters (and many of our own supporters). There really is a "culturally anxious America"[100] out there. They may be mostly White and mostly older, but not all of them are.[101] And there are a lot of these people (more than we realize and in places we don't recognize), and our arrogance in dismissing their anxiousness as simple racism has cost us dearly. Racism is obviously deeply involved for many people, but it's foolish to think of that as the only thing. The impulse to hold on to what you have, to protect it, is a very human feeling. It's no different in emotion from wanting to protect your home and family. In fact, that is exactly how a lot of conservative voters see it.

---

99 In this case, the Oxford Dictionary, but they all say some version of the same thing.

100 Thank you, Cornell Belcher.

101 Take a careful look at the makeup of the 2020 Trump voters.

Playing on this cultural anxiety is the essence of Republican strategy. It's exactly what Make America Great Again was all about. The appeal of MAGA wasn't about America as a superpower or a manufacturing giant. That's not what excited so many people and drove them wild at rallies, or caused so many millions who didn't go to rallies . . . who shuddered at the very idea of the rallies . . . to go on and vote for Trump.[102] MAGA was a subconscious message that the stability and security of the lives they used to know could somehow be recaptured. It didn't matter how unpleasant Trump was as a person. It didn't matter that his promises were pie in the sky, that all of it was blatantly impossible. It captured them because that's what so many of them wanted to believe. Of course it drew in racists. It drew in all the racists, but it drew in a heck of a lot of others as well. It drew in Hispanics and more than a few Black voters. In short, it worked. And it's going to go on working until we start looking at what's really going on.

The Republican strategy isn't about politics at all, it's about culture. The Republican goal is to keep us separated into two warring tribes based almost entirely on cultural differences. They want everyone who lives in a big city to think that anyone who lives out in the

---

102 These are the same people we kept talking about, asking, "How could they?"

country is an ignorant racist . . . a MAGA supporter . . . because then they can convince those folks that everyone who lives in the big city is an elitist, socialist snob, bent on destroying their way of life.

The Republican Party has an objective here: to turn the entire country into Whole Foods versus Cracker Barrel on a deeply emotional level, because then they can smoothly lump together a whole lot of independent voters with the haters. Then they can make them all feel like a tribe, emotionally connected . . . and threatened . . . in a very primal way when they shouldn't be at all.

And so many of us have played right into their hands. So many of us in the big cities . . . especially activists . . . have watched all those images of MAGA rallies on TV and done exactly what the Republican Party wants us to do: give everything from pickup trucks to NASCAR a political label.

The truth is, what you drive, what you watch, and where you shop says nothing about what kind of a person you are as an individual. Absolutely nothing. Neither does the size of your city or town, or where it's located. It does, however, say a lot about your lifestyle. It's a big indicator of what kinds of things you're used to . . . the things you've been exposed to. It also says a lot about the kinds of language you're accustomed to hearing, the things that make you listen.

Rural areas . . . and smaller cities[103] . . . may be where the Republican base is located, but it's also where the people who we want to bring over to our side live. And it's home to huge numbers of loyal Democrats, people who embrace the basic values we're talking about in this book but who live in a world with a different style, different language, and different day-to-day priorities.

That's what the elite who guide our language and messaging keep missing . . . confusing lifestyle with substance. Pressing the latest politically correct language on an issue isn't how we expand support. Getting directly to the issue itself is. And addressing the issue with universal values, language common to us all, is how we do it. Missing this point is why our messaging so often sucks, why we keep losing . . . and let's be clear: for us, winning 51 percent of the vote is losing. We may take the presidency, we may control the House and the Senate, but we will never gain our real goals . . . things like true universal health care and actual campaign finance reform . . . until we have the kinds of majorities in both chambers that make that kind of real reform possible, and that won't happen until we reach out and embrace that significant part of the Republican vote . . . that part of "cul-

---

103 The US Census defines "urban" as either 2,500 or 50,000, depending on how you look at it. The truth is towns and cities are on a continuous spectrum from tiny to giant. There is no sharp dividing line.

turally anxious America" . . . that is not, in their hearts, fundamentally tied to racism and all the prejudices that go hand in hand.

⋅

OK, but what about *real* conservative principles? They exist, right? There are still sincere Republicans out there, aren't there? What about the ones who didn't follow Trump into the wilderness? What do they believe? What do they mean when they talk about these things?

The quick answer is "small government" and "fiscal responsibility." Those are the words that keep rolling off their lips. And they may mean it. But when you peel things back and try to pin down the truth, it isn't so easy. Because the truth keeps changing. And it has been, ever since 1776.

The Founding Fathers saw themselves as motivated by the Enlightenment. They were educated people. They read and they argued ideas, sophisticated ideas, but in reality, they and their brethren were the conservatives of their day. They were the elite of their time. Many were quite wealthy,[104] and it's a fact that a lot of them didn't actually believe in democracy at all, not the way we think of it. They saw the common man . . . the great unwashed (you and me) . . . as incapable of making

---

104 See *Business Insider*, July 4, 2020: "Many of the Founding Fathers Were Incredibly Wealthy."

wise decisions, incapable of governing. These particular Founders felt that only wealthy (White) men were entitled to rule.[105] It's the very European concept of a privileged class,[106] and it's that class attitude that kept most of us from getting the vote for so long. It's that same attitude that's the ultimate origin of Jim Crow and voter suppression and gerrymandering, and it's exactly why we're stuck with the Electoral College.[107]

Not all the Founding Fathers felt that way. New England was a hotbed of participatory democracy[108] and there were some violent arguments over the principle of "one man, one vote," but in the end, the wealthy got their way.

But the Republicans' modern reimagining of conservative principles and their origins doesn't stop here. Republican would-be ideologues adore promoting these same Founding Fathers as icons of general wisdom on just about everything. When you need a rationale, be it on religion or culture or even health insurance, turn to

---

105 The essence of Goldwater's philosophy.

106 For Europeans, it's about your family bloodlines. Our way is much simpler: money and race, and increasingly, just money.

107 And we will stay stuck with it until Democrats control two-thirds of the Senate and two-thirds of all the state houses. Not any time soon.

108 It's no accident that New Englanders and their New York cousins basically started the Revolutionary War.

the Founding Fathers. If you listen to the Republicans, these wise men of old foresaw the future, foresaw virtually everything, and their profound wisdom should still guide us today, holy writ.[109]

The Founders certainly displayed real foresight about human nature and politics. They created the oldest functioning democracy in the world. They set up institutions that have endured for more than two centuries, and that's a truly incredible accomplishment. Bravo, Founders!

But general wisdom and foreseeing the future?[110] How could they? Nobody knew what an airplane was back then. Nobody even thought flying was possible. Nobody imagined a car, or huge trucks moving millions of tons of cargo out to a coast most people didn't even know was there. FedEx didn't exist. Neither did computers or cell phones or the idea of people in space. The Founders also couldn't conceive of women having an equal voice (let alone serving as soldiers), or the idea of modern medicine and all the technology that goes with

---

109 This is the origin of originalism, the conservative constitutional idea that we should follow the strict intent of the Founding Fathers . . . whatever that might be. Interesting to note that originalism only really became a thing during the administration of Ronald Reagan.

110 Or even the near future. Among other things, these Founding Fathers were the same people who promptly sold the navy and virtually disbanded the army, only to have to rebuild both a short time later.

it, or any form of modern communication that didn't involve a horse or a hand-powered printing press. To say that the Founding Fathers conceived of the world we live in, that they anticipated all the problems inherent in modern life, is ridiculous. It's equally ridiculous to say they could conceive of what would be needed to deal with these problems . . . the very role of government itself.

The truth is, the modern Republican concept of conservative values didn't begin with the Founding Fathers, it began in 1933, and it was a knee-jerk reaction to FDR. The wealthy industrialists of those days . . . what would now be called the Billionaire Class . . . were appalled at the reforms Roosevelt was undertaking. The ultrarich saw the New Deal as a direct threat to their power, to their enormous profits and political influence. To these privileged few, things like a forty-hour workweek and an end to child labor were not about the betterment of human lives, it was about curtailing their ability to literally do as they pleased.

So the rich pulled together a lot of their favorite politicians and organized a fight. The politicians and their academic friends quickly came up with two basic ideological positions to stand on: limited government and fiscal responsibility,[111] the twin tenets of conservatism. These ideas sound good, and they're easy to remember (and who can argue with being responsible with money?). The words caught on, serving as the twin pillars of conservative principles right on through the sixties. Republican ideologues expounded endlessly on these principles in books and papers,[112] ending with Barry Goldwater and *The Conscience of a Conservative*.[113]

But then the Republican Party actually took power.[114] Nixon arrived, and Reagan . . . especially Reagan . . . and those principles fell apart. Not as messaging, of course. They still hyped them . . . they still do . . . but the reality of governing quickly put an end to the twin tenets.

Fiscal responsibility was the first to go. Ronald Reagan increased the national debt by 186 percent. Yes,

111 Which meant a balanced budget back in those days, which meant limited spending, which meant limited government, which meant limits on the regulation of corporations. It's a circle.

112 If you're curious about the ideological underpinning of modern conservatism, take a look at Friedrich Hayek's *The Road to Serfdom* or Russell Kirk's *The Conservative Mind*. If you really want to get to the emotional origins of utopian capitalism, read some Ayn Rand . . .

113 The first two chapters of Goldwater's book are worth a read (they can be easily downloaded for free). They lay out the reasoning behind the principles of utopian conservatism . . . which is basically Libertarianism.

114 Once again, exempting Eisenhower and his distinctively un-Republican ways.

186 percent.[115] George W. Bush is next, raising the debt by 101 percent.[116] They simply needed more money to keep governing, and to project their political power. They couldn't raise taxes, not after the hype they'd gotten elected on, so they did what all modern Republican presidents have done . . . they borrowed the money. They took out the national credit card, spent what they needed, and left it for someone else to deal with . . . the proverbial kicking of the can down the road.[117] And of course, the next Republican president to appear after the Bushes was the self-proclaimed "King of Debt" himself, Donald Trump.

Small government went out the door just as fast. Spending all that money meant having someone to do the spending. Despite all the Republican rhetoric at election time, "the government" kept on growing, and it still does.

And, of course, Newt's Death Star Philosophy ended any actual moral conservative tenets left over from the

---

115 Roughly. See, among others, thebalance.com and treasurydirect.gov.

116 Same.

117 Ronald Reagan is the original "borrow and spend" Republican, which makes his rather effective labeling of us as "tax and spend" Democrats while he was running up all that debt rather ironic. And, of course, the only president to actually lower the debt was Clinton.

Rockefeller days.[118] Once the Republicans consummated their marriage to the segregationists and the evangelicals and all the others who came on board, any semblance of traditional conservative principals became ancient history. The real issues of the day for Republicans rather quickly became guns, abortion, homophobia, Christianity under attack, fear of immigration, and fear of Black Americans . . . all of it wrapped up in a flag that said "Conservative Principles."

Unfortunately for the Republicans there are no principles that cover all these things, and morality, at the same time. There is no moral ethic that covers the fierce defense of individual freedom that also empowers the government to control a woman's body (and forces states to follow suit). There is no political principle that covers smaller government and expanding the military at the same time, no philosophy that covers both mounting debt and fiscal responsibility, or the dignity of the individual and racism.

And so in the era that started with Reagan, Republicans as a whole left the original conservative ideology behind and drifted into vague definitions of it, which

----

118 A real apology to all those sincere Republicans (the "Never Trumpers," the Lincoln Project, and all the rest) who grew up on the idea of conservative values and still believe that the ideas of limited government and fiscal responsibility somehow still represent the Republican Party. Sorry, but everything you're reading here is true.

was essentially no definition at all. It became whatever seemed to suit the moment, all of it liberally sprinkled with Newt-words like "freedom" and "liberty."

So what's left? If all the traditional conservative principles have been discarded, what ethic has kept the Republican Party on this course of damaging their own people with such endless fervor?

There is one underlying conservative principle that we have yet to talk about. It is the only principle that has never changed, not once in nearly a century. It's unspoken. It's denied vigorously by every single Republican . . . adamant, indignant denials that roll feverishly off their lips . . . but this principle underlies everything the Republicans have done since 1933. And it most definitely underlies everything that's going on now. It's the GOP's own Prime Directive: support for the wealthy class . . . boosting the rich . . . something they've managed to disguise brilliantly while engaging in it endlessly.[119]

One can argue it's not that simple, but actually it is. Support for the rich is right there at the heart of everything, and you don't need a poster boy like Donald Trump to see it. All you have to do is take that one idea as a starting point, then look at how it applies to everything that's gone on for more than eight decades.

---

119 Convincing millions of middle- and working-class folks that they are being helped by giving money to the wealthy is brilliant.

Protecting the rich is why the GOP keeps pushing huge tax cuts for the wealthy.[120] It's the origin of Reagan's "supply-side economics" (also called "voodoo economics"), the idea that if you pour lots of money into the hands of the rich, some of it will slip through their fingers and "trickle down" to you and me.[121]

Protecting the rich is why Republicans oppose things like the Environmental Protection Agency and the Consumer Protection Agency, why they oppose any kind of regulation of clean air or water, why they want to open our natural resources to unlimited exploitation and why they oppose any sort of research into the consequences of it. Rich people own the coal mines. They own the giant corporations that pollute the water and soil. They own the banks and financial institutions that make enormous profits off this sort of thing.

Protecting the rich is why they oppose Social Security[122] and Medicare, and expanding Medicaid. It's why they oppose all social programs, the very ones that would benefit a lot of their base: Social programs cost money. And money means taxes, and taxes ultimately

---

120 While endlessly denying it.

121 Ever wonder why no one proposes giving a trillion-dollar tax cut just to us middle-class people, letting our spending trickle up to the rich?

122 Not openly, of course, because it's too popular now. They just propose shrinking it or privatizing it into destruction.

put a damper on profits. Social programs are also politically dangerous, at least to the wealthy.

None of this is about "capitalism," and none of it is about "socialism." That's a bill of goods the Republicans have been trying to sell for a long time. And it's not about free enterprise or the entrepreneurial spirit or small businesses. This is about one thing: the abuse of power. It's about giving billions in tax breaks and shady deals to wealthy donors while diverting public outrage to welfare cheats. It's about insider trading and being in bed with lobbyists. It's about secret meetings with wealthy donors and making promises that never see the light of day. It's about the swamp, the very real swamp, the very thing that outrages all those people who consider themselves the Tea Party.[123] And that leads us to the other Republican Party.

THE DARK EMPIRE

Does 130 billionaires sound like a lot? That's how many we had in 1995 . . . 130 separate individuals, each one owning more than $1,000,000,000. By 2010, that number had jumped to more than four hundred. Today,

---

123 We're not innocents in this either, and it's the very
reason we need to lead with our core values and force
our politicians and donors to live up to them.

Republican

If you're a long-time Republican and you're reading this and shaking your head in disbelief, think about something. Racism exists. Poverty exists. Homelessness exists. What does the Republican Party propose to fix these things? What real-life legislation does it propose right now to fix voting rights or discrimination against women? When was the last time you heard a major Republican politician stand up and say, "Enough! Hunger cannot stand. We must do something about it now!"?

Democrats do it all the time, have for a very long time. So, where are the Republicans in all this? Where is the outrage, the demand for action? Where are the Republican politicians marching in the streets against racism? Where is the legislation to expand voter rights, or the plan to give everybody real health care, or the bill to end homelessness? Where, ask yourself, is the Republican Common Thread?

If you're an old-style Rockefeller Republican, if you still believe in both small government and racial justice, fiscal responsibility and ending hunger . . . if you believe in facts and morality . . . then sadly, you no longer have a party. But if our basic values appeal, if they seem to hold true, you are welcome to join us. There is a lot to do, and it's a very big tent.

there are more than six hundred[124] of these people. Of course, there have always been billionaires, but what's going on today in the billionaire class is something else, wealth and excess not seen since the Gilded Age that preceded FDR.

It's easy to miss these folks. Billionaires don't walk around the mall. They don't shop at Whole Foods, either. (Actually, they don't shop at all. They have other people to do that for them.) Billionaires live in huge mansions surrounded by security, and they fly on private jets to their yachts in the Caribbean. We ordinary people may not see them, but they're there, and they have tremendous influence over what happens.

The uber-rich have always had their hands in politics (after all, it's how an awful lot of them became uber-rich). Financing politicians . . . and outright buying them . . . has gone on since the beginning of politics itself, and it continues today, more than many of us would like to believe. And we're not immune. The Democratic Party has plenty of dark personalities we'd rather forget, corruption plain and simple.[125] Modern Republican politicians have plenty of these uber-rich in their stable, but

---

124 And we're not counting "hundred-millionaires" or even "ten-millionaires," though they're part of all this as well, the "1 percent" you're always reading about.

125 And ones who do good as well. It's no accident you know who George Soros and Tom Steyer are.

How much?!

It's worth taking a moment to ponder what "a billion dollars" actually means. If you take brand-new $100 bills, stack them up nice and tight, you need a good inch to get $10,000. An inch. One billion dollars fills giant crates and weighs more than eleven tons (22,000 pounds). Put another way, one billion dollars equals 19,000 years of tuition at Harvard, or four thousand Lamborghinis . . . or someone who makes $50,000, working for 20,000 years.

More to the point: If you're that same working stiff making $50,000 a year, and you feel strongly enough about a candidate to make a $100 campaign donation . . . it's the same as one billionaire giving $2,000,000. Something to remember when you read about those $100,000-a-plate campaign events and wonder who on earth is shelling out that kind of money for a dinner.

The top 1% of this country is worth $10 million each, and that's an average that includes their wives, their kids, and their little babies. The bottom half of this country . . . over 150 million people . . . averages about $42,000 each. And of course, the top 1% own half of the stock market. That's half of all stocks being owned by 1% of the country. Together with the "almost uber-wealthy" (the top 10% of Americans) they own more than 80% of the stock market . . . the answer to why the stock market seems so disconnected from Main Street.

what has formed in the shadows in recent decades is something else entirely . . . literally a parallel Republican Party.

It started small. Billionaires like Joseph Coors[126] and John Olin[127] (and Richard Scaife and Lynde and Harry Bradley) decided they wanted to do more than just buy politicians. Lot of ambitious GOP operatives were always hovering nearby, buzzing around the money and whispering in their ear, and pretty soon things like an embryonic Heritage Foundation sprang into being, along with special programs at prestigious law schools to teach the billionaire, "free enterprise" way of looking at the law.[128]

But the Dark Empire really began when Charles and David Koch arrived on the scene.[129] Their genius was to think big. They realized the real answer to getting their way was simple: control the actual elections themselves. And their plan was just as simple in theory: build an empire of organizations capable of gaining that kind

---

126 Yep, the brewing tycoon, also known as a supporter of the John Birch Society and once described as "a little bit right of Attila the Hun." He was also the man who tried to make the faculty of the University of Colorado take a loyalty oath.

127 Arms and chemicals fortune.

128 Olin started out by "sponsoring" (paying) any law professor who would express his particular conservative point of view. It worked, and so Olin and his people began offering the actual law schools millions of dollars if they would agree to set up a

of influence and make the whole thing self-funding and self-perpetuating.

It took a while, but in time, the Kochs were instrumental in establishing giant organizations such as the Heritage Foundation and the Cato Institute, growing them from fringe outfits into accepted mainstream organizations that regularly place spokespeople on national TV. Each of these Goliaths was (and is) run independently by a properly conservative staff (independent, but still dependent on the Koch's money). In time, each one became an independent, self-perpetuating source of right-wing energy. And sure enough, in time, each one began spinning off more self-perpetuating organizations.

To pay for all this, the Koch's established a consortium of like-minded, right-wing billionaires to cough up a steady stream of moola. Other billionaires started their own operations, the US Chamber of Commerce chipped in, and thanks to Citizen's United and a host of other

---

program to teach these ultraconservative views. Harvard had no trouble taking $10 million. Yale, Columbia, Cornell, Georgetown, and a bunch of others followed suit and presto, Olin's extreme philosophy became legitimate, something any student could choose to study at prestigious law schools all over the country.

129 The Koch brothers have a total net worth somewhere in the area of $100 billion (that's tuition for 1,900,000 years at Harvard), a fortune that stems largely from fossil fuels. David Koch was an active partner in their political undertaking until he died in 2019.

legal decisions (which the Koch empire helped pass), much of this money became anonymous. No one ever needed to know who gave it or who got it. We still don't.

These organizations form a complicated, rarely seen network. They employ legions of ideologues and writers who produce endless position papers . . . and actual legislation . . . for Republican politicians to use. They produce vast amounts of op-ed pieces for local and national media, and they testify before Congress as "expert witnesses." They sponsor all-expense-paid junkets for Republican politicians and their families to fabulous resorts where these elected officials get to mingle . . . out of sight, of course . . . with selected lobbyists and operatives while enjoying their vacation. They pay for lavish seminars where billionaires and politicians (and even Supreme Court justices) get to mingle, and their operatives provide cadres of instant demonstrators in populist garb, ready to show up whenever they're needed to create a "spontaneous" demonstration.

All of this, every bit of it . . . including smearing everything they oppose with the word "socialism" . . . is carefully crafted to justify one thing: more money for the 1 percent.[130]

---

130 Whatever else is on the surface, the end goal is always promoting the lowering of taxes on the rich and the elimination of oversight on corporations.

Utopian Capitalism

Utopian capitalism is what the billionaire class mostly believes in. It's not an actual term that you'll see in print, but it's very much their ideology, and . . . without ever admitting it publicly . . . the Republican Party has embraced this philosophy as justification for their policies.

Utopian capitalism is a magical place where enlightened billionaires . . . men gifted with superior morality and social wisdom . . . rise naturally to the top of society. There, they stand tall in this imagined world, America's best. Gifted with superior morality and social wisdom (despite the greed that got them there), and freed from all of society's troublesome laws and regulations, these wise men naturally do what's best for the country, ensuring liberty and prosperity for everyone else while raking in more billions.

It's a pretty theory on paper, but it's as utterly false as utopian communism. Both have been tried in real life, and both have failed. One leads to dictatorship by government, the other to dictatorship by wealth . . . a path we are dangerously close to following.

During recent decades, these people have brought you things like the Federalist Society, the ultraconservative legal organization that ensures each Republican president has a list of proper conservative judicial candidates to choose from.[131] These people have also brought you the American Conservative Union and CPAC, the yearly convention where all GOP politicians go to pay obeisance to the wealthy and prove their conservative bona fides (and search for donors).

The Dark Empire is real. It's powerful beyond what most of us can imagine, and it can no longer be dismantled.[132] Yet another thing we Democrats have let happen.

Here's the good news: there is no shadow Democratic Party. There *are* semisecret donor get-togethers. There are lobbyists and special interest groups flashing money all over the place, but there is no secret organization behind the scenes pulling our strings. There is no Democratic dark empire for one simple reason: our core values don't help the wealthy make money.[133] We have no

---

131 Supreme Court justices approved by the Federalist Society include Scalia, Alito, Thomas, Gorsuch, Kavanaugh, and Barrett.

132 Not until major campaign finance reform passes both houses of Congress. Not anytime soon.

133 Once again, it's not that simple, but it is. Democratic politicians have sold out to special interests since forever. It hasn't been because of our core values, but in spite of them.

ideology that aids the rich in their quest for power. In fact, we have no ideology at all. We have beliefs, core values to aspire to, and those values are about helping people, about making America a better place to live in for regular folk. None of these beliefs are about raking in billions of dollars.

There are uber-rich who openly support us, but they don't do it because it's a path to increasing their wealth. For the most part, they do it because they, too, believe. They do it because they, too, worry about the country. Republicans will tell you that their billionaires believe as well, and they do. The difference is what they believe.

Myths and Fables

★

There's a deeper problem that the Republicans have created, one we're mostly not even aware of. The demonizing is easy to see, the labeling almost as easy. But the myths they've created, the false truths they've managed to implant into our national culture over the years— those are a lot harder to come to terms with. They are false assumptions, each and every one of them, clever definitions that have been slipped into our national discourse so often and so smoothly that Americans have come to accept them as truth. Us, too.

These myths are all about values, basic emotional concepts that are easy to visualize, easy to grab onto. And accepting these myths guides people effortlessly into making false choices. They are myths that serve one master: the billionaire class.

Here are a few to think about:

Capitalism is good.
Have you ever really thought about it? "Capitalism" is actually a meaningless word politically because it only

describes economics. All it says is that private companies own the factories.[134] Every major country in the world is capitalist . . . the good ones and the very bad ones. France and all those union strikes you keep reading about? Capitalist.[135] Canada, with its popular health care system? Capitalist. Even Communist China is half-capitalist at this point[136] (the Shanghai Stock Exchange is the fourth-largest stock market in the world).

And if you find yourself still clinging to the idea that somehow capitalism itself must be inherently good politically, that . . . somehow . . . it must represent freedom and democracy, consider this: the oligarchs in Putin's Russia, the country that's hacking our elections and pointing nuclear weapons at us—they're all capitalists. Nazi Germany was capitalist . . . Hitler, concen-

---

134 Capitalism is an economic system. It means private companies do the producing. The United States has worked that way since colonial days and it always will. The New Deal didn't change that one iota. Neither did LBJ and the Great Society, and neither will any new policy that comes down the line. Corporations will be making automobiles and designing computers forever. It's just reality.

135 France is actually the sixth largest economy in the world.

136 The opposite of capitalism isn't socialism, it's communism, and communism is dead. It's gone, a footnote to history. The existence of North Korea, Cuba, and Venezuela just emphasizes the "dead" part. So does the fact that no one calls China "Communist China" anymore.

tration camps, et al.[137] So was slave society in the Old South. Those plantation owners with their beautiful mansions down in Dixie were full-blown capitalists. So were the slave markets they went to.

Being "capitalist" doesn't say anything at all about how a country is run politically or morally (sorry, it doesn't say anything "bad," either). It doesn't have anything whatsoever to do with democracy or freedom or justice (or access to health insurance). It just means private companies produce and distribute cars a hell of a lot better than the government.

This myth that capitalism is some kind of absolute cultural value . . . the "goodness" of America . . . has been around since Reagan, since way before that. What they're talking about, of course, is utopian capitalism. That fanciful idea is the underlying rationale for every bit of the uber-rich agenda, and it's something we've failed to address . . . failed to even recognize properly . . . since the death of the Roosevelts.

Socialism is bad (really bad).
Socialism is another meaningless word, yet it's the bane of our existence. It *is* a word—you can look it up in the dictionary—but unless you're a political science profes-

---

137 Even the ovens were capitalist-made. J. A. Topf and Company not only made crematoria ovens, it also made ventilation systems for the gas chambers at Auschwitz II–Birkenau.

sor at some university, socialism has lost any practical meaning. Does it mean communism? Or does it mean Social Security and Medicare? How about the right to clean air and clean water? Is that "socialist"? Or national standards to ensure fair voting in elections?

The truth is, the Republicans have turned the word "socialist" into a bogeyman,[138] a label they can stick on anything they don't like to make it seem evil. Over time, they've managed to make socialism a word that now conjures up Ultimate Darkness to a lot of Americans and causes distinct uneasiness in most of the rest. The mere fact that we Democrats immediately start defending ourselves when faced with the label is evidence enough.

Socialism won't have a neutral meaning for a long, long time, and those of us who go on defending it, trying to explain its nuances, are making a big mistake. Reagan put it rather eloquently: "If you're explaining, you're losing." If you're defending, you're losing, too.

Defending also means we've fallen into their trap. When we defend, it means we've accepted their false choice, that it all comes down to capitalism versus socialism. But that isn't the choice at all. There are lots of choices, and few of them involve the ideals of capitalism or socialism.

---

138 And they're working hard on "liberal."

We're never going to clean up the word "socialist" and make it usable politically, and we need to quit trying. This isn't about truth in semantics, it's about the public's long-term emotional perception of the words, and we've already lost that battle. It's over. What we need to do instead is ignore it. We need to change the conversation. Instead of even talking about capitalism and socialism, we need to present Americans with real choices, choices about values. If most Americans believe clean water is a fundamental right, then sooner or later, policies will happen. If affordable health care is a recognized right, the only argument possible is how to implement it. This is how we need to approach it. Our values have to dictate how we get to our policies, not the other way around.

Government is bad.

Well, the government is bad at running an economy, manufacturing things. The communists proved that rather effectively, and you'd have to go pretty far out on the fringe to find anybody in this country who thinks the government should build cars.

Fixing the economy, fixing the problems, that's a different story altogether. America's economic power isn't based on capitalism, it's based on free enterprise. Forget all that billionaire nonsense that free enterprise[139] isn't "free" if billionaires aren't free to cheat and pollute and create monopolies. Free enterprise is like a football game. It only works if there are rules and referees . . . government rules and regulations.

Ah, but "Power corrupts . . ." That's what the Republicans like to toss around to prove how bad government is. It's a great saying,[140] but what the Republicans conveniently forget to mention is that money corrupts just as surely as political power.[141] And large corporations are all about money. Their job is to produce profit—as much as possible, as fast as possible. There is absolutely nothing in the corporate world about moral responsibility; that's another Republican myth.[142] Does anyone think that the drug companies were thinking about moral responsibility when they were setting drug prices? Or pushing oxycodone? Or that health insurance companies were thinking about morality when they refused to

---

139 Free enterprise, free markets, entrepreneurship, private enterprise . . . they all mean the same thing in real life: private companies in open competition.

140 ". . . and absolute power corrupts absolutely" is the rest of the saying.

141 Money is probably more corrupting. Politicians are never free of competing pressures . . . voters, lobbyists, and the like. Billionaires are as free as it gets. The truly rich live a life where no one around them ever says "no."

142 And the exceptions prove the rule. As Google is investigated and their workers protest, remember that their original motto was, "Don't be evil."

cover preexisting conditions before Obamacare forced them to?[143]

Large corporations aren't immoral, they're amoral.[144] If doing good turns a bigger profit, they do good. If doing bad creates a bigger profit . . . and no one enforces rules . . . they do bad. And we've already seen what happens when corporate greed meets no rules and no referees: inhumane work conditions, starvation wages, and child labor, culminating in the Great Depression.[145] In fact, corporate greed is the very reason we came into existence as a political party.

The point of all this is that we're not socialist and we're not capitalist . . . we're Americans who are trying to make this a better country to live in. The point is, capitalism is a foundation of our economy, something that is necessary but most definitely in need of regulation.

---

143 Or coal companies that scrimped on safety measures? Or chemical companies that contaminated local drinking water? The list is endless.

144 Note that we're talking about corporations, not small businesses. Privately owned small businesses are a different ball game altogether. Sweeping them all together—saying what's good for one is good for the other—is another Republican myth.

145 And that leaves out the modern incarnations such as contaminated water, polluted air, thalidomide, the Love Canal, or the financial crisis of 2007 and 2008, when unregulated banks almost brought down the world's economy.

The battle over this basic concept . . . rules and regulations for corporations, a level playing field to ensure competition and protect the public interest . . . has already been fought and won, but the Republicans have been incredibly successful in trying to fight it all over again. And we've let them. We've let them make this about raw capitalism instead of about values and the national good.

We need Americans to understand that the real issue isn't the size of government, it's the use of government. As Democrats, we need to be clear that we don't believe in big government, and we don't believe in small government. We believe in government that gets done what's needed, when it's needed. Nothing more and nothing less. That's what we've got to make clear to people (and to ourselves): **we stand for an effective government based on values that help people**.

Fighting racism is somehow a liberal thing (racism, or xenophobia, or homophobia, you name it).
This is the biggest myth of all. There's nothing "Democrat" about being for human rights. Human rights aren't about the Left or the Right,[146] they're about being American. **Human rights are basic values, the very core of our existence as a nation**. There's nothing "Democrat"

---

146 They certainly aren't about capitalism versus socialism. Just take a look at Hitler (capitalist) versus Stalin (communist) and what that meant for civil rights.

about being for universal health care either, or free elections, or a free press. They're basic American values.[147] And if you don't support those basic values . . . publicly . . . shame on you. And shame on us if we don't make them a public issue.

•

Undoing all these myths is an incredibly important part of where we need to go, but we're not going to undo them by defending, or explaining, or attacking. We fight these false ideas by changing the conversation, by making it about values, by focusing on basic goals. We undo these myths by making them irrelevant, by . . . step by step . . . making the whole Republican way of politics irrelevant.

Their entire strategy for the past fifty years is tied to one idea: turning everything into "us" versus "them."[148] For the Republicans to win . . . the Republican Party, the Dark Empire, the White supremacists, all of them . . . America always has to be divided into warring tribes,

---

147 Most of the values in this book are American values, something both parties ought to be supporting. One day, Democrats and Republicans may actually agree on these values. Then the arguments will just revolve around "how."

148 The Republican Party has always needed an enemy to make their real objectives work. For a long time, it was communism. Then the communists disappeared and it morphed into socialism, which is still alive and kicking. But it took the Death Star philosophy and the twisted charisma of Donald Trump to come up with the best enemy of all, the one that will never go away or be defeated . . . us.

tribes that are based on perceived cultural differences, on a primal emotional identity, an anger that makes logic irrelevant, that makes even facts irrelevant.

And they've succeeded. They've managed to take people who shouldn't identify with each other and make them believe they are one, and they've done it by getting all these people to forget their differences . . . and facts . . . and unite behind a sense of perceived cultural unity, of being a righteous group whose very existence is under siege. The core of this group, its very beginnings, may be racist in nature, but the Republican operatives have managed to expand that vision to include everyone who is uneasy about the enormous social changes underway in this country, everyone who cannot comprehend many of the things that are happening to them . . . regardless of their views on racial justice, and often in spite of their views. Basically, the Republican Party has managed to emotionally unite every White person who feels left out or left behind in America.

And we have helped the Republicans. We have bought into the idea that it's us and them, that things are either left or right, liberal or conservative, right or wrong. It's the assumption that our endless goal is to win that thin slice of America that tips us to 51 percent. It's the same subconscious idea that a lot of us cling to that demographics will fix everything, that we just need to wait for the babies.

And when we accept these assumptions, we also accept leaving "them" out . . . all the people we need to bring over. It's how we have so easily forgotten about the very real people who lost the manufacturing jobs, the communities that have watched their very way of life disappear. And we *have* forgotten. Much as we don't want to admit it, we have moved on in our language and thinking . . . big-city thinking, elitist thinking . . . and suddenly remembering those people at election time . . . suddenly coming up with a jobs message to appeal to the Rust Belt . . . doesn't change a thing. Our messaging, our obsession with policies and purity, our very way of talking, says it all.

That's our real enemy, that tribal way of thinking . . . theirs *and* ours . . . and we don't fight it by doing the same thing over and over, by using the same thinking, the same tactics. And we don't do it by attacking "them" as a group. Attacking them is exactly what the Republicans want. It's what they need, what they depend on, along with anything else they can use to separate us, anything whatsoever that says there is a "we" and a "they" . . . especially if it says there's a "we" and a "they" inside our own party.

The Republican Party's biggest nightmare is us waking up to what's really going on, because if we finally get our act together, if we finally realize this is all about values . . . our values of justice and opportunity versus their values of threat and fear . . . then their reign is over. This isn't 1950. It isn't even twenty years ago. It's now, and right now . . . despite all the noise and confusion . . . a majority of Americans inherently recognize our core values. This majority definitely doesn't recognize all our messages or our policies . . . *we* don't recognize all our policies . . . and these same Americans definitely don't recognize the labels we've let ourselves be tagged with. But things like the principles of justice and opportunity . . . fair play . . . that they do understand. Not everybody, that's for sure, but a lot more than 51 percent . . . and that's our future, bringing those people on board.

Creating change isn't our real challenge. Creating consensus is, the kind of national consensus that makes real change possible. That needs to be our number one goal: **creating a significant majority in America that emotionally identifies with basic American values**. We need to drive people away from the subconscious artifacts of fear and threat that the Republicans have constructed, the very same artifacts that Donald J. Trump drove home so spectacularly, the artifacts that threaten our democracy itself. That's our job: waking people up . . . us included . . . and the first step is establishing our fundamental unity of purpose, our universality of purpose . . . our basic values themselves.

The Democratic Creed

(A work in progress . . .)

★

- We believe all people are created equal, that this is America's fundamental ideal.

- We believe that America is a democracy, by and for the people: ruled by the Constitution and its interpretations, protected by the Bill of Rights, and inspired by the Declaration of Independence.

- We believe these founding documents demand Freedom, Justice, and Opportunity for all Americans, in full and equal measure . . . regardless of who you are, what you believe, or where you live.

- We believe that the Duty of government is to strive endlessly to make the ideals of Freedom, Justice, and Opportunity a reality for all.

- We believe that the Purpose of government is to protect our nation, defend our democracy, and to endlessly promote the welfare of each and every one of us.

- We believe that fighting for these ideals is our purpose as a political party.

WE HOLD THESE THINGS
TO BE SELF-EVIDENT:

Freedom means...

- The right of every citizen to shape their own life, and their beliefs ... so long as it does not infringe on the rights or safety of others.
- The free flow of information and movement.
- The right to privacy.
- Free and fair elections, at every level, in every place in America:
- Elections that are fully transparent.
- Elections that are free of the role of wealth and the wealthy.
- Elections that guarantee unlimited and easy access to voting for every American citizen.

Justice means...

- A society where every citizen is safe in their person and their home, and their day-to-day lives.
- A society where every citizen is treated with dignity, regardless of race, creed, or personal difference of any kind.
- A society where every citizen is treated equally before the law, and by the law.
- A society where racism is wrong, where discrimination is wrong, where the government intervenes

when racism or discrimination threatens a person's basic rights.

Opportunity means . . .
- Every American deserves an equal chance to pursue their dreams, to be judged on their ability and their effort alone.
- Every American, child and adult alike, deserves the education that gives them that chance.
- Every American adult deserves the chance to earn a living wage, and to work with dignity . . . a job where pay, working conditions, and treatment are suitable reward for the effort and skill put in.
- Every American deserves to live without fear of hunger or homelessness or lack of medical care. These things are not only rights, they are America's moral duty to provide.
- Every American deserves to live in a healthy environment that includes clean air, clean water, and safe food.
- Every American deserves the chance to move forward: no one left out by change, and no one left behind ... no matter who they are or where they live.

We further believe that American democracy depends on . . .
- A free and independent press, dedicated to truth and objectivity.

- An educated citizenry with free and easy access to information.
- A nation that accepts and embraces diversity.
- Full financial transparency in election campaigns, in political office, and in government transactions.
- An American economy based on Free Enterprise, and protected by the government from the baser instincts of large corporations and the financially powerful.
- The continued existence of a strong military, free of political involvement and financial corruption, and dedicated to protecting us against all enemies foreign and domestic.
- Educators and law enforcement officers being treated as among the most important parts of society, highly paid and stringently selected, and meeting exacting national standards of professionalism, ethics, and psychological motivation.
- American citizens who care. Without this, nothing is possible.

This is what we believe.

Tomorrow . . .

★

This is *our* creed. These are our values . . . each and every one of us who cares about the Democratic Party . . . and so we need to make this creed our own. It isn't enough to just read a proposal here, no matter how many people worked on it. We . . . you and I and everyone else . . . need to take this creed apart line by line and think about it. We need to revise it where necessary, hone every sentence . . . and not just the creed . . . we need to go after every idea in this book. We need to take each idea aside and test it, talk it over until there's not only a consensus but a sense of ownership, a sense that it's truly ours.

And we need to do it now. The biggest crisis we face as Democrats isn't politics, it's affirming our identity, achieving a unity of purpose, a clear sense of fundamental direction for the next twenty years. And that sense of where we want to go is about much more than our party. It's about everything Trump and the GOP have done, everything we've played into. It's about five decades of looking the other way as the Republicans implemented their Death Star Philosophy. It's about alternative facts and the storming of the Capitol. It's about racism and xenophobia and anti-Semitism. It's about the threat to basic justice and free elections, and economic opportunity for the forgotten. Our public statement of belief has to be about all of this, everything we've struggled with . . . and been frustrated by . . . for so very long.

Go back and look at the first page of this book. As much as we've accomplished over the years as Democrats, as much good as we've done, we've been an abject failure at defining ourselves. No one knows who we really are. No one knows what we stand for. Instead of creating a firm identity, we've stood back over the years and let the Republicans do it. We've let them label us as socialists and Marxists and enemies of the people . . . leaving us to go on defending and explaining endlessly.

Aren't you tired of it? Aren't you sick of being cloaked in someone else's lies and phony labels?

And it's so simple. Our core values are powerful. Our basic beliefs go directly to the fundamental beliefs at the heart of the Declaration of Independence. They are literally enshrined in the United States Constitution itself. All our creed really has to do is convey that in direct, no-nonsense English, something devoid of politics, something that doesn't even hint at policies. Our creed needs to ring true to everyone, not just to us, but to the very people outside our party we need to convince as well. If we do this right, our creed will excite. It will reach out to the American people and grab them by the throat. It will say these are not just Democratic values, these are American values. It will say these values are for all of us, and these values are right.

And once we have it proclaimed, we need to make it clear that our creed . . . our Democratic creed . . . is the basis for everything we do. Our messaging, year in and year out, has to begin and end with this creed. When the issue is health care, we need to start with the idea that health care in America is a right. We need to make sure everyone understands that America accepting that is the real issue, the only true barrier to making it happen.

When the issue is economic opportunity, we need to start with the idea that education is a right, that access to the internet is a right, that clean air and water to live by is a right. We need to stand on rights and values above all else. We need to be the ones proclaiming those rights and values, and leave the Republicans to do the defending.

And that means us, you and me. This isn't something to be passed down by the Democratic National Committee. It's not something to be decided by a few people in Washington. This needs to evolve at the grass roots and be passed up. Our creed needs to come from us, the people who make up the party, all of us . . . moderates and progressives, big-city folk and people in the heartland, Blacks and Whites and everyone in between. It's something that needs to be argued out by every single one of us . . . Democrat to Democrat . . . then passed up for the leaders in Washington to pay attention to.

Establishing our creed is the first step, but truly fixing things is about you and me. It's about the emotions we conjure up in the everyday people we know, the ones who don't have time to follow politics. This is about our friends and neighbors, the words and symbols we use with them. This is about persuasion, separating the people with good hearts from the haters, turning 51 percent of the vote into 61 percent, and more. This is about you and me and endless conversations with the people around us, conversations that set off emotional reactions, that cause people to finally say, "I knew that. I just didn't realize it." This is about getting a real majority of America on board with the basic ideas of a just society . . . in every sense of the word.

The Trump era did one good thing for us: it created an incredible amount of grassroots energy inside our party. We need to seize on that energy, each and every one of us who believe in this thing called the Democratic Party, each and every one of us who really believe there is a Common Thread and a Prime Directive. We need to organize informally. We need to have dinners, talk over drinks, start book clubs, even just hang out at Starbucks. We need to start endless discussions over ideas . . . all of us . . . discussions about the issues and their impact on our day-to-day lives.[149]

We need to make the party feel like us again, and in the process, create an antidote to the overwhelming noise and confusion modern life has sunk us into.

In the end, this is about fixing the country, setting things right. "The last great experiment for promoting human happiness"[150]—those were George Washington's words about the American Revolution a long time ago, but he got it a bit wrong. The American Revolution was certainly the starting point, but the Great Experiment is actually going on right now, all around us. Ready or not, we happen to live at that precise moment in history when it's finally becoming possible to take the ideals this country was founded on and apply them to everyone. Right now . . . today, and for the tomorrows to come . . . that's the true test of those words we aspire to in the Declaration of Independence. And we are the ones being tested . . . Democrats and Americans alike. What happens next is up to us.

---

149 See what follows.

150 Washington's letter to Catherine Sawbridge Macaulay Graham, January 9, 1790. The actual quote contains a comma after "experiment."

Ten questions we need to ask ourselves

★

1. Are we more than a political party? Should we be?

2. Do we actually have core values, values and ideals we all share?

3. Does the Democratic Creed represent those values?

4. Do we really have a Prime Directive as a party? Do we really have a moral purpose?

5. Do we have a clear vision of what we want to ultimately achieve?

6. How do you see the Democratic Party? Does the American public see it the same way?

7. What defines a Democrat?

8. Can you make a difference? Do you want to?

9. What can you do to continue this conversation with other Democrats?

10. What can you do to start this conversation with other Americans?

NOTES & IMAGE CREDITS

Page 19, note 4: https://bit.ly/3reqbnF

Page 20, note 7: See *Sundown Towns: A Hidden Dimension of American Racism* by James W. Loewen

Page 21: Lynching of Thomas Shipp and Abram Smith. Marion, Indiana, August 7, 1930. Photograph by Lawrence Beitler (cropped). Courtesy of the Indiana Historical Society.

Page 35: Bogalusa, Louisiana, July 1, 1965. Photograph by Matt Herron. © 1976 Matt Herron / Take Stock / TopFoto

Page 52, note 47: Full text at www.pbs.org, June 24, 1978

Page 54, note 50: *National Journal*, October 23, 2010

Page 70, note 71: https://www.forbes.com/pictures/ fgdi45edlde/the-mostpowerful-businesswomen- in-the-world/?sh=39ecb2fa7002

Page 72, note 76: https://prn.to/33crFW8

ACKNOWLEDGMENTS

Writing *Democrats 101* was no small task. It's a short piece, but finding ways to take so many ideas and put them together in an easily accessible manner without sacrificing any of the underlying truth required a lot of thinking, and rethinking.

It also took the skill and passion of the large number of people who were involved in editing and getting the thinking right. It can't be said enough: the words in this book are the author's, but the ideas and vision belong to a lot of people. The list of people is rather large (and growing), but here are a few:

My wife, Isabelle Broyer. Without her there is no book. Period. Karen Gravelle for her endless editing and encouragement, going back farther than I care to remember. Sabrina Duncan and the Indiana book club who have helped form me as a writer. Karen Duncan, and Josh and Nat Board, who read and reread and did so much to get the thinking straight. Forest Ingram in Oregon for all his input, Mark Melnick who has contributed so much more than design, and finally the folks at Plainwords Press, the people who changed this from a book into a national message, especially Abby Diess and everything she did, and Dave Broadway, who has been much more than the Director of Communications. There are more, many more than can be listed here. A sincere thanks to all of you. I may be the author, but the message in this work belongs to all of us.

J.M. will be heard from again, soon. So will all the people that help shape J.M.'s words.

RESOURCES

For further discussion
What other work (films, documentaries, books, and the like) do you think would complement this conversation? Please share your ideas with us:

Website
PlainWordsPress.com

Twitter
@PlainWordsPress

•

Book clubs
Questions for discussion, by chapter, are available for download at PlainWordsPress.com.

Further support is available upon request.

ABOUT THE AUTHOR

J.M. Purvis is a transplanted Midwesterner who loves good coffee, talking with friends, and rooting (hopefully) for the Knicks. He is also a military veteran (combat), a former journalist, and currently teaches at New York University. J.M. has watched this country change for a very long time, both politically and culturally. He has watched the enormous social progress that has resulted, uneven and often unsure, but always there. He has watched the Reaction as well, the forces opposed to change that are trying so hard to force us back.

2016 was a catalyst, a moment that led him to the realize that America had arrived at a crossroads, a moral turning point much bigger than politics and elections, and that if we Democrats . . . the only real party left . . . don't grasp that, the country is in trouble. He waited patiently for someone else to write about it, to produce something in the vein of *Common Sense*, but no one did. And so *Democrats 101* was born.